MW01630569

cabin cooking

WILLIAMS-SONOMA

cabin cooking

Good Food for the Great Outdoors

Recipes by
Tori Ritchie

Photography by
Chris Shorten

WELDON
OWEN

WILLIAMS-SONOMA
Founder and Vice Chairman Chuck Williams
Book Buyer Victoria Kalish

WELDON OWEN INC.
Group Publisher, Bonnier Publishing Group John Owen
CEO and President Terry Newell
Senior VP, International Sales Stuart Laurence
VP, Sales and New Business Development Amy Kaneko
Director of Finance Mark Perrigo
VP and Publisher Hannah Rahill
Production Director Chris Hemesath

Consulting Editor Norman Kolpas
Design Concept Patty Hill
Design Kari Perin, Perin + Perin
Food and Prop Stylist Heidi Gintner
Assistant Food Stylists Kim Konecny, Judith Wadson

In Collaboration with Williams-Sonoma
3250 Van Ness Avenue, San Francisco, CA 94109

A WELDON OWEN PRODUCTION

415 Jackson Street, San Francisco, CA 94111

First Published in 1998
10 9 8 7 6 5 4 3 2 1

ISBN-13: 978-1-74089-942-0
ISBN-10: 1-74089-942-3

Printed in China at 1010 Printing International Ltd

A NOTE ON WEIGHTS AND MEASURES

All recipes include customary U.S. and metric measurments. Ametric conversions are based on a standard developed for these books and have been rounded off. Actual weights may vary.

A NOTE ON NUTRITIONAL ANALYSIS

Each recipe is analyzed for significant nutrients per serving. Not included in the analysis are ingredients that are optional or added to taste, or are suggested as an alternative or substitution either in the recipe or in the recipe introduction. In recipes that yield a range of servings, the analysis is for the middle of that range.

the environment

Your cabin's environment can provide you with a bounty for the table, including fish from local lakes or streams and wild berries. Check ahead with area authorities to learn what foods are safe and in season, and what, if any, legal limits there might be on catching or gathering them. To help maintain a pristine environment, be sure to pack out any trash and recyclables you brought in.

Escape. This word alone sums up the allure of cabin life. Whether the cabin is sheltered in the woods or looks out on a lake, stream, or meadow, it brings us blissfully close to nature. Preparing food at a cabin, though, can carry responsibilities. Remember that respecting the environment is paramount.

A Note on High-Altitude Cooking

If your cabin is above 3,000 feet (1,000 meters), you'll need to adjust some recipes to compensate for the reduced air pressure, which makes liquids boil at lower temperatures and causes breads and cakes to rise higher and faster. Generally, a few simple adjustments can help counteract these effects: reduce baking powder and soda by ⅛–¼ teaspoon per 1 teaspoon; decrease sugar by ½–1 tablespoon per 1 cup (8 oz/250 g); add 1–2 tablespoons more liquid per 1 cup (8 fl oz/250 ml); and increase baking temperatures by 15–25°F (8–10°C).

introduction

"There is pleasure in the pathless woods,
There is a rapture on the lonely shore,
There is society, where none intrudes,
By the deep Sea, and music in its roar:
I love not Man the less, but Nature more."
– LORD BYRON

gathering at the table

Fresh air and recreation conspire to whet appetites for cabin-cooked meals. From the first sip of morning coffee that precedes a hearty breakfast to the last drop of hot chocolate that caps a satisfying dinner, good food and drink taste all the more delicious when enjoyed with nature close at hand.

Setting the Dining Scene

It doesn't matter how elegant or humble your cabin's furnishings and accessories are. Nature is the primary theme, and at every turn your surroundings can provide you with ample inspiration for creating memorable dining experiences. Whether you set the table with simple plastic dishes, old enamelware from a local antique shop, or a favorite set of china that's been retired to the country, the touches of nature that you bring to the table will set a relaxed, convivial tone.

Take advantage of a beautiful day or night at your cabin to eat alfresco, moving a table outdoors if necessary. Gather wildflowers, shapely branches, pinecones, or other objects to decorate the table. Even the day's catch can provide impromptu visual interest before you clean and cook it. Don't forget votive candles or lanterns for nighttime dining, including citronella candles or lamps to ward off insects.

the cabin pantry

If you own a cabin, it's a good idea to stock the kitchen with a full range of basic ingredients and versatile cookware and utensils. Many pantry items can be stored long-term. Refrigerate preserves, syrups, condiments, and pickles and check expiration dates regularly. Store oils and vinegars, dried beans, pastas, and rice in airtight containers away from heat and light, and check them regularly for freshness. Keep dried herbs, breakfast grains, flours, and canned goods in a pantry or cupboard and replace them annually.

The best strategy for stocking a cabin pantry and kitchen is to plan ahead. Decide what you'll want to cook, then make lists of necessary ingredients as well as indispensable equipment, such as a chef's knife, a paring knife, a saucepan, a heavy frying pan, a spatula, and wooden spoons. Check against an inventory of items on hand at the cabin to arrive at a final list of what you'll need to bring along.

Planning and Packing

When choosing your cabin menus, plan to use perishable items such as tender produce, seafood, poultry, and ground meats early in your stay. Reserve hardier ingredients such as root vegetables, apples, citrus fruits, whole cuts of meats, and cured meats for later meals. Consider preparing foods that will provide more than one meal. A turkey breast, for example, once roasted for dinner, will yield leftovers for sandwiches or pot pies. When packing food to bring, use an ice chest for perishables that must be kept cool. Put frozen foods or packets of artificial ice on the bottom and stack other items on top, ending with the most fragile items.

WEDGEWOOD

beverages

sun tea with mint cubes

1 small bunch fresh mint
4 cups (32 fl oz/1 l) cold water, plus water for ice cubes
2 tea bags, black, herbal, flavored, or a combination
sugar (optional)
lemon slices

Place a mint leaf in each compartment of 2 ice cube trays. Fill the trays with water, then freeze.

Pour the cold water into a lidded 1-qt (1-l) clear glass container. Place the tea bags in the water, leaving the strings dangling over the side. Cover and set in direct sunlight for at least 1 hour, or for up to 3 hours. Let steep until the tea is a good, strong color.

Remove the mint ice cubes from the trays and place in a large pitcher or individual glasses. Pour in the steeped tea, discarding the bags. Add sugar to taste, if desired, and garnish with lemon slices.

serves four to six | per serving: calories 2 (kilojoules 8), protein 0 g, carbohydrates 1 g, total fat 0 g, saturated fat 0 g, cholesterol 0 mg, sodium 6 mg, dietary fiber 0 g

fresh honey lemonade

⅓–½ cup (4–6 oz/125–185 g) honey
1½ cups (12 fl oz/375 ml) steaming hot water
1 cup (8 fl oz/250 ml) lemon juice
ice cubes
fresh mint sprigs (optional)
lemon slices (optional)

In a heatproof 1-qt (1-l) measure or bowl, combine the honey and hot water and stir until the honey is dissolved. Stir in the lemon juice. Let cool for at least 10 minutes or cover and refrigerate until ready to serve.

Pour over ice. If desired, garnish with mint sprigs and/or lemon slices.

serves two to four | per serving: calories 161 (kilojoules 676), protein 0 g, carbohydrates 44 g, total fat 0 g, saturated fat 0 g, cholesterol 0 mg, sodium 19 mg, dietary fiber 0 g

summer sangria

2 cups (16 fl oz/500 ml) orange juice
⅓ cup (3 oz/90 g) sugar
1 bottle (24 fl oz/750 ml) white wine
½ bottle (12 fl oz/375 ml) red wine
1 cup (8 fl oz/250 ml) sparkling water
ice cubes
2 oranges, thinly sliced

In a large pitcher, stir together the orange juice and sugar until the sugar is dissolved. Add the wines and stir well. If desired, cover and refrigerate for up to 8 hours or until ready to serve.

To serve, add the sparkling water, ice cubes, and orange slices and stir well. Pour into individual glasses.

serves six to eight | per serving: calories 204 (kilojoules 857), protein 1 g, carbohydrates 26 g, total fat 0 g, saturated fat 0 g, cholesterol 0 mg, sodium 8 mg, dietary fiber 1 g

rich hot chocolate

2 cups (16 fl oz/500 ml) whole or low-fat (2 percent) milk

⅓ cup (2 oz/60 g) semisweet (plain) chocolate chips

1 teaspoon vanilla extract (essence)

In a small saucepan, combine the milk, chocolate chips, and vanilla. Cook over medium heat, stirring once or twice, until the milk is just steaming, 3–5 minutes. Continuing to cook, beat with a wire whisk or a rotary beater until the chocolate is melted and the mixture is frothy. Pour into mugs and serve.

serves two | per serving: calories 288 (kilojoules 1,210), protein 9 g, carbohydrates 30 g, total fat 16 g, saturated fat 10 g, cholesterol 34 mg, sodium 120 mg, dietary fiber 0 g

mulled cider

4 cups (32 fl oz/1 l) pure, unsweetened apple cider

2 cinnamon sticks, broken in half

about 15 whole cloves

6–8 pieces crystallized ginger, 1 oz (30 g) total weight

½ cup (4 fl oz/125 ml) dark rum or bourbon (optional)

1 apple

juice of ½ lemon

In a small, heavy saucepan, combine the cider, cinnamon, cloves, and crystallized ginger. Warm over medium-high heat until the cider is steaming; do not allow to boil. Reduce heat to medium-low and continue to cook for about 10 minutes. Remove from the heat and, if desired, stir in the rum or bourbon.

Peel and slice the apple, then moisten the slices with lemon juice to keep them from discoloring. Strain the cider into mugs and float 3 apple slices on top of each serving.

serves four | per serving: calories 163 (kilojoules 685), protein 0 g, carbohydrates 41 g, total fat 0 g, saturated fat 0 g, cholesterol 0 mg, sodium 13 mg, dietary fiber 1 g

spiced pinot noir

1 bottle (24 fl oz/750 ml) pinot noir or other dry red wine such as zinfandel or merlot

½ cup (4 oz/125 g) sugar

4 orange zest strips

1 tablespoon whole allspice berries

1 teaspoon whole black peppercorns

In a heavy saucepan, combine the wine, sugar, zest, allspice, and peppercorns. Stir over medium-high heat until the sugar is dissolved and the wine is steaming; do not allow to boil. Reduce the heat to medium-low and cook for about 10 minutes. Remove from the heat and ladle into mugs or heatproof glasses to serve.

serves four to six | per serving: calories 192 (kilojoules 806), protein 0 g, carbohydrates 26 g, total fat 0 g, saturated fat 0 g, cholesterol 0 mg, sodium 8 mg, dietary fiber 0 g

breakfast

raisin bread french toast with sautéed pears

For the best flavor, use Comice or Anjou pears. You can also substitute a good cooking apple. Brown Sugar Bacon (page 25) alongside makes this a substantial country breakfast.

3 tablespoons unsalted butter
2 firm, ripe pears, cored and cut into chunks (see note)
¼ cup (2 fl oz/60 ml) orange juice
6 eggs
½ cup (4 fl oz/125 ml) milk
¼ teaspoon ground cinnamon
¼ teaspoon sugar
pinch of ground nutmeg (optional)
8 slices raisin bread
about 1 cup (8 fl oz/250 ml) maple syrup, warmed

Melt 1 tablespoon of the butter in a large frying pan over medium-high heat. Add the pears and cook, stirring, until just softened, about 3 minutes. Pour in the orange juice, raise the heat to high, and cook, stirring, until the liquid reduces to a glaze and the pears are soft, about 4 minutes. Remove the pears and their sauce from the pan and keep warm while you make the french toast. Wipe the pan clean and set aside.

In a large shallow bowl, beat together the eggs, milk, cinnamon, sugar, and nutmeg, if using. Place 4 slices of the bread in the egg mixture and let soak for about 2 minutes, turning once.

In the same frying pan over medium-high heat, melt 1 tablespoon of the butter. Working with 4 slices at a time, transfer the soaked bread to the pan and cook, turning once, until golden brown, about 4 minutes total. Transfer to a plate and keep warm. Then soak and cook the remaining 4 bread slices, using the remaining 1 tablespoon butter.

Divide the french toast among warmed plates, and top evenly with the pears and their sauce. Pass the maple syrup at the table.

serves four | per serving: calories 613 (kilojoules 2,575), protein 15 g, carbohydrates 97 g, total fat 20 g, saturated fat 9 g, cholesterol 346 mg, sodium 321 mg, dietary fiber 4 g

oatmeal griddle cakes with pecan-maple syrup

Homemade pancakes don't take much longer to make than those prepared from a mix, and they are far tastier and healthier. Top them with nuts, syrup, and yogurt for an unforgettable start to any day (photo at right).

1 cup (3 oz/90 g) rolled oats
1¾ cups (14 fl oz/430 ml) buttermilk
⅔ cup (3 oz/90 g) chopped pecans
1 cup (8 fl oz/250 ml) pure maple syrup
1 cup (5 oz/155 g) all-purpose (plain) flour
3 tablespoons firmly packed light brown sugar
2 teaspoons baking soda (bicarbonate of soda)
pinch of salt
1 egg, at room temperature, lightly beaten
4 tablespoons (2 oz/60 g) unsalted butter, melted, plus butter as needed
½ cup (4 oz/125 g) low-fat plain or vanilla yogurt

In a large bowl, combine the oats and buttermilk and let stand for about 15 minutes. Meanwhile, in a small saucepan, toast the pecans over medium heat, stirring often, until fragrant and lightly browned, about 5 minutes. Remove from the heat and pour in the maple syrup (the mixture will bubble up); stir well. Cover to keep warm and set aside.

In a small bowl, stir together the flour, brown sugar, baking soda, and salt. Add to the soaked oats, then stir in the egg and 2 tablespoons of the melted butter. Mix well.

In a frying pan over medium-high heat, heat the remaining 2 tablespoons melted butter. Ladle the batter, about ¼ cup (2 fl oz/60 ml) at a time, spaced well apart, into the pan. Cook until the tops are bubbly and the bottoms are golden brown, about 4 minutes. Turn and cook until golden brown on the second side, about 3 minutes longer. Transfer the pancakes to a plate; keep warm. Repeat with the remaining batter, adding more butter if needed.

Divide the pancakes among individual plates and top each serving with some of the pecan-maple syrup and a spoonful of yogurt. Pass the remaining pecan-maple syrup at the table.

makes about twelve pancakes; serves four to six | per pancake: calories 263 (kilojoules 1,105), protein 5 g, carbohydrates 38 g, total fat 10 g, saturated fat 3 g, cholesterol 31 mg, sodium 275 mg, dietary fiber 2 g

brown sugar bacon

This recipe (photo page 23) has all of two ingredients and is so addictive that you'll wonder why you haven't always made bacon this way. If you don't have a slotted broiler pan, you can fry the bacon in a nonstick frying pan, sprinkling the sugar over it about halfway through cooking.

8 strips thick-cut bacon, about ¾ lb (375 g) total weight

3 tablespoons firmly packed light brown sugar

Preheat a broiler (griller). Line the bottom of a slotted broiler pan with aluminum foil.

On a sheet of waxed paper or foil, arrange the bacon strips side by side. Press the brown sugar through a sieve with the back of a spoon, letting it shower over the bacon strips and distributing it as evenly as possible. Rub a fingertip over each strip to smooth out the sugar and press it into the bacon.

Transfer the strips to the slotted top of the broiler pan, twisting each strip several times to form a corkscrew as you lay it down. The strips can be close together but should not touch. Broil (grill) 6 inches (15 cm) below the heat until the edges are browned and crisp, 5–7 minutes; watch carefully as the sugar can burn. Turn and broil on the second side until crisp, 2–3 minutes longer. Transfer to paper towels to drain. Serve warm.

serves four | per serving: calories 176 (kilojoules 739), protein 7 g, carbohydrates 10 g, total fat 12 g, saturated fat 4 g, cholesterol 20 mg, sodium 384 mg, dietary fiber 0 g

mixed mushroom omelet

This oversized omelet makes a hearty breakfast for two. A nonstick pan will give you the best results; if you have only a regular skillet, use more butter or just scramble the eggs and top them with the mushroom-onion mixture and sour cream.

½ lb (250 g) mixed mushrooms such as button, cremini, shiitake, or chanterelle
1 large portobello mushroom
2 tablespoons unsalted butter
½ yellow onion, sliced
1 teaspoon fresh thyme leaves or ½ teaspoon dried thyme
4 eggs
2 tablespoons warm water
2 tablespoons thinly sliced chives or green (spring) onion tops
salt and ground pepper
¼ cup (2 oz/60 g) sour cream

Wipe the mushroom tops clean with a damp cloth; remove and discard the stems and slice the caps. Cut the portobello slices in half crosswise. Place an 8- to 10-inch (20- to 25-cm) nonstick frying pan over medium-high heat and melt 1 tablespoon of the butter. Add the onion and cook, stirring, until softened, about 7 minutes. Add the mushrooms and thyme and continue to cook, stirring often, until the mushrooms are soft and any liquid has evaporated, about 8 minutes. Remove the mushrooms and onion from the pan and keep warm. Wipe the pan clean and set aside.

In a bowl, beat the eggs with the warm water and chives; season with salt and pepper to taste. Melt the remaining 1 tablespoon butter in the same frying pan over medium-high heat. Pour the egg mixture into the pan. When it begins to set, use a wooden spoon to push the edges gently toward the center, tilting the pan so that the uncooked egg flows underneath. Continue until the eggs are almost set but still slightly moist on top, about 3 minutes.

Spoon the mushroom-onion mixture over half of the omelet; top with the sour cream. Shake the pan to loosen the omelet; if it sticks, loosen the edges with the wooden spoon. Starting with the mushroom-covered side, slide onto a warmed plate. When half of the omelet is on the plate, invert the pan to fold the omelet over the filling. Cut in half and serve at once.

serves two | per serving: calories 380 (kilojoules 1,596), protein 18 g, carbohydrates 16 g, total fat 28 g, saturated fat 14 g, cholesterol 469 mg, sodium 152 mg, dietary fiber 3 g

canadian bacon hash with poached eggs

Canadian bacon makes for a lean and flavorful hash. For extra convenience, boil the potatoes the night before. If poaching eggs seems too complicated, you can top the hash with fried eggs. Accompany with Old-Fashioned Buttermilk Biscuits (page 31).

3 red potatoes, about 1 lb (500 g) total weight
2 tablespoons unsalted butter
2 tablespoons vegetable oil
½ lb (250 g) sliced Canadian bacon, cut into 1-inch (2.5-cm) pieces
4 green (spring) onions, including tender green tops, thinly sliced
3 stalks celery, thinly sliced
1 red or green bell pepper (capsicum), seeded and diced
½ teaspoon dried thyme
salt and ground pepper
vinegar as needed
4 eggs
chopped fresh parsley (optional)

Place the potatoes in a saucepan and add cold water to cover. Cover and bring to a boil over high heat. Uncover and cook until the potatoes are just tender when pierced, about 20 minutes. Drain the potatoes and let cool (or refrigerate overnight). Peel and cut into 1-inch (2.5-cm) pieces; set aside.

In a large frying pan over medium-high heat, melt the butter in the oil. Add the Canadian bacon and cook, stirring often, until the bacon begins to sizzle and is lightly browned, about 5 minutes. Add the green onions, celery, bell pepper, and thyme and continue to cook, stirring often, until the vegetables have softened, about 4 minutes. Add the potatoes and cook, stirring often, until potatoes are heated through, about 4 minutes (longer if potatoes were refrigerated). Season to taste with salt and pepper.

Meanwhile, fill a sauté pan three-fourths full of water; add several drops of vinegar and bring to a boil. Reduce the heat to a bare simmer. Crack each egg into a small bowl or cup, then slide carefully into the simmering water. Cover and poach the eggs until the whites are firm and the yolk sacs have thin veils of white, 4–6 minutes, depending on your taste. Spoon the hash onto individual plates and top each serving with a poached egg. Sprinkle with parsley, if desired.

serves four | per serving: calories 381 (kilojoules 1,600), protein 21 g, carbohydrates 25 g, total fat 22 g, saturated fat 7 g, cholesterol 256 mg, sodium 901 mg, dietary fiber 3 g

oatmeal with dried cherries and almonds

Steel-cut and Irish oats, which have more heft and a nuttier flavor than rolled oats, make a delicious slow-cooked porridge. If you prefer regular rolled oats, use the amount of liquid called for on the package, substitute milk for half of the water, and cook as indicated.

3 cups (24 fl oz/750 ml) water
2 cups (16 fl oz/500 ml) low-fat milk
pinch of salt
⅓ cup (2½ oz/75 g) firmly packed light brown sugar
1 teaspoon vanilla or almond extract (essence)
1 cup (6 oz/185 g) steel-cut or Irish oats (see note)
1 cup (6 oz/185 g) dried cherries, coarsely chopped if large
1 tablespoon unsalted butter (optional)
¼ cup (1 oz/30 g) sliced (flaked) almonds
about 1 cup (8 fl oz/250 ml) milk, cream, or buttermilk

In a saucepan over medium-high heat, bring the water, 2 cups (16 fl oz/500 ml) milk, and salt just to a boil. Add the sugar and vanilla or almond extract, stirring until the sugar is dissolved. Stir in the oats and dried cherries. Return to a boil and stir until the mixture starts to look foamy, about 1 minute, then reduce the heat to low and simmer uncovered, stirring often, until the oats are cooked through but still chewy, about 30 minutes. Do not overcook; the oats should still have a little bite.

Stir in the butter, if desired, and let the oatmeal stand, covered, for 5 minutes. Spoon into individual bowls. Sprinkle each serving with sliced almonds, and accompany with milk, cream, or buttermilk.

serves four | per serving: calories 482 (kilojoules 2,024), protein 14 g, carbohydrates 87 g, total fat 11 g, saturated fat 4 g, cholesterol 18 mg, sodium 135 mg, dietary fiber 5 g

old-fashioned buttermilk biscuits

Enjoy these delicious biscuits (photo page 29) warm from the oven, split open and slathered with butter and honey.

2 cups (10 oz/315 g) all-purpose (plain) flour
2 teaspoons sugar
2 teaspoons baking powder
½ teaspoon baking soda (bicarbonate of soda)
½ teaspoon salt
½ cup (4 oz/125 g) chilled unsalted butter, cut into small pieces
1 cup (8 fl oz/250 ml) buttermilk

Preheat an oven to 425°F (220°C). In a bowl, stir together the flour, sugar, baking powder, baking soda, and salt. Using a pastry blender or 2 knives, cut in the butter until the mixture resembles coarse meal. Pour in the buttermilk and mix quickly with a fork until blended. Turn out onto a lightly floured work surface. Gather the dough together, then knead briefly until it just holds together.

Roll the dough into a circle about 8 inches (20 cm) in diameter or into a rectangle about 8 inches (20 cm) long. Cut into biscuits with a floured 3½-inch (9-cm) cutter or the rim of a large juice glass, or, using a knife, cut the rectangle in half crosswise, then cut each half into 4 pieces. Arrange the biscuits about 1 inch (2.5 cm) apart on an ungreased large baking sheet. Bake until golden brown and puffy, about 15 minutes. Remove from the oven and let cool on the baking sheet for about 5 minutes. Serve warm.

makes about eight biscuits; serves four to six | per biscuit: calories 257 (kilojoules 1,079), protein 5 g, carbohydrates 31 g, total fat 12 g, saturated fat 8 g, cholesterol 33 mg, sodium 355 mg, dietary fiber 1 g

huevos rancheros

for the salsa:

2 large, ripe avocados

4 green (spring) onions, including tender green tops, minced

¼ cup (2 oz/60 g) canned diced green chiles

juice of 2 or 3 limes

3 tablespoons minced fresh cilantro (fresh coriander)

salt

for the huevos rancheros:

2 cans (15 oz/470 g each) black beans, drained and rinsed

warm water as needed

salt and ground pepper

8 eggs

4 green (spring) onions, including tender green tops, thinly sliced

¼ lb (125 g) feta cheese, crumbled

1 tablespoon unsalted butter

4 corn tortillas

To prepare the salsa, pit and peel the avocados. In a bowl, mash the avocados well with a fork. Stir in the green onions, chiles, juice from 2 limes, and minced cilantro. Season to taste with salt and more lime juice, if desired. Cover with plastic wrap and set aside for up to 30 minutes.

Meanwhile, prepare the huevos rancheros: In a small saucepan over medium heat, combine the black beans with a few tablespoons of warm water, just enough to moisten the beans. When the beans are hot, mash lightly with a fork to break them down and thicken them. Season to taste with salt and pepper. Cover the beans and remove from the heat.

Preheat a broiler (griller). In a bowl, beat the eggs with 2 tablespoons warm water. Mix in the green onions and feta cheese. Melt the butter in a large frying pan over medium-high heat. Add the egg-cheese mixture and softly scramble. While the eggs are cooking, place the tortillas on a baking sheet and broil (grill) about 4 inches (10 cm) below the heat, turning once, until just lightly browned, about 3 minutes total.

Place the tortillas on individual plates and spread evenly with the mashed black beans. Top with the scrambled eggs and the salsa, then serve.

serves four | per serving: calories 642 (kilojoules 2,696), protein 29 g, carbohydrates 48 g, total fat 40 g, saturated fat 12 g, cholesterol 458 mg, sodium 931 mg, dietary fiber 10 g

cornmeal waffles with blueberry-orange syrup

The nooks and crannies of these crisp waffles trap a delicious homemade fruit syrup. The waffles can be cooked, cooled, layered with waxed paper in a plastic bag , and frozen for up to 1 month; then just pop the sections into a toaster to reheat.

for the blueberry-orange syrup:

¾ lb (375 g) blueberries (fresh or thawed frozen)

¼ cup (2 oz/60 g) sugar

juice of 1 orange

¼ teaspoon ground cinnamon

for the waffles:

1 cup (5 oz/155 g) all-purpose (plain) flour

1 cup (5 oz/155 g) yellow cornmeal

2 tablespoons sugar

1 tablespoon baking powder

pinch of salt

1½ cups (12 fl oz/375 ml) milk

1 egg, at room temperature, lightly beaten

3 tablespoons unsalted butter, melted, plus butter as needed

To make the syrup, combine the blueberries, sugar, orange juice, and cinnamon in a saucepan. Stir well. Bring to a boil, then reduce the heat to low and simmer, uncovered, until slightly thickened, about 8 minutes. Remove from the heat and set aside.

To make the waffles, preheat a waffle iron. In a large bowl, stir together the flour, cornmeal, sugar, baking powder, and salt. In another bowl, beat together the milk, egg, and 2 tablespoons of the melted butter. Pour into the flour mixture and stir until combined.

Grease the waffle iron with the remaining 1 tablespoon melted butter. Ladle the batter, about ½ cup (4 fl oz/125 ml) at a time, onto the waffle iron and cook according to the manufacturer's directions until golden. Transfer the waffles to a plate; keep warm. Repeat with the remaining batter, adding more butter if needed. Divide the waffles among individual plates, top with the blueberry-orange syrup and serve.

makes eight 6-inch (15-cm) waffles; serves four to six | per waffle: calories 278 (kilojoules 1,168), protein 6 g, carbohydrates 47 g, total fat 6 g, saturated fat 4 g, cholesterol 46 mg, sodium 234 mg, dietary fiber 2 g

mountain breakfast scones

To earn their name, these cakelike scones come in mountainous proportions. For smaller scones, cut the dough rectangle in half to form two squares, then cut each square on the diagonal into quarters. Serve the smaller scones with tea or coffee in the afternoon.

1½ cups (7½ oz/235 g) all-purpose (plain) flour
3 tablespoons plus 1 teaspoon sugar
2 teaspoons baking powder
pinch of salt
¼ cup (2 oz/60 g) chilled unsalted butter, cut into small pieces
⅓ cup (2 oz/60 g) golden raisins (sultanas)
¾ teaspoon grated orange or lemon zest
⅔ cup (5 fl oz/160 ml) plus 1 tablespoon milk
1 teaspoon ground cinnamon

Preheat an oven to 425°F (220°C). In a bowl, mix together the flour, 3 tablespoons sugar, baking powder, and salt. Using 2 knives or a pastry blender, cut in the butter until the mixture resembles coarse meal. Mix in the raisins. Stir the zest into the ⅔ cup (5 fl oz/160 ml) milk. Make a well in the center of the flour mixture and pour the milk into it; mix quickly with a fork until moistened.

Turn the dough out onto a lightly floured work surface and gather together. Knead briefly just until the dough holds together; do not overknead or the scones will be tough. Pat the dough into a rectangle about ½ inch (12 mm) thick, 4 inches (10 cm) wide, and 8 inches (20 cm) long. Starting with a short side, fold the dough in half to make a square. Press the dough lightly so that the top adheres to the bottom. Cut the square on the diagonal into quarters; you will have 4 big triangular scones. Transfer to an ungreased baking sheet, spacing them about 2 inches (5 cm) apart.

In a small bowl, stir together the 1 teaspoon sugar and the cinnamon. Brush the tops of the scones with the 1 tablespoon milk and sprinkle evenly with the cinnamon sugar. Bake until the scones are puffed, but not dry, about 15 minutes. Remove from the oven and let cool on the baking sheet on a rack for about 5 minutes. Serve warm or transfer to the rack and let cool completely.

makes four large scones | per scone: calories 409 (kilojoules 1,718), protein 8 g, carbohydrates 65 g, total fat 14 g, saturated fat 8 g, cholesterol 37 mg, sodium 303 mg, dietary fiber 2 g

summer squash frittata

In this flat, Italian-style omelet, the filling is mixed in with the eggs. If crookneck and pattypan squash are unavailable, substitute 3 medium zucchini.

2 tablespoons olive oil, plus oil as needed
3 small pattypan squashes, diced
2 small yellow crookneck squashes, diced
2 tablespoons chopped fresh oregano or 1 tablespoon dried oregano
salt and ground pepper
6 eggs
2 tablespoons warm water
3 oz (90 g) fontina or Monterey jack cheese, cut into small pieces

In a heatproof 8-inch (20-cm) frying pan over medium-high heat, warm the 2 tablespoons olive oil. Add the diced squashes and cook, stirring occasionally, until softened and lightly browned, about 8 minutes. Stir in the oregano and season to taste with salt and pepper.

Meanwhile, preheat a broiler (griller). In a small bowl, lightly beat the eggs with the warm water, then stir in the cheese. When the squash is ready, spread it in an even layer in the frying pan; if the pan seems dry, add a little more olive oil. Pour in the egg-cheese mixture. When it begins to set, lift the edge with a wooden spoon to let the uncooked eggs flow underneath. Continue to cook until the top of the frittata looks fairly dry, about 4 minutes.

Slip the pan under the broiler, placing it about 6 inches (15 cm) below the heat. Broil (grill) until the top of the frittata is puffed and golden, about 3 minutes. Cut into wedges and serve directly from the pan.

serves four | per serving: calories 298 (kilojoules 1,252), protein 16 g, carbohydrates 6 g, total fat 23 g, saturated fat 8 g, cholesterol 343 mg, sodium 266 mg, dietary fiber 1 g

puffed oven pancake with summer fruit

Based on an old recipe for German pancakes, this dish is a one-pan marvel. The batter is baked over sliced peaches or nectarines and berries in a frying pan and dusted with sugar to serve. It's delicious with steaming mugs of hot coffee or Rich Hot Chocolate (page 19).

½ cup (2 oz/60 g) all-purpose (plain) flour
2 tablespoons granulated sugar
⅓ cup (3 oz/80 ml) milk
3 eggs
¼ cup (2 oz/60 g) unsalted butter
2 firm, ripe peaches or nectarines, peeled, if desired, pitted, and sliced
1½ cups (6 oz/185 g) raspberries or blackberries
about 2 tablespoons confectioners' (icing) sugar
lemon wedges (optional)

Preheat an oven to 425°F (220°C). In a bowl, beat together the flour, granulated sugar, milk, and eggs until thoroughly blended. Set aside.

In a 10- to 12-inch (25- to 30-cm) heatproof frying pan over medium-high heat, melt the butter. Add the peaches or nectarines and cook, stirring often, until the fruit is hot and slightly softened, 3–5 minutes, depending on ripeness. Remove from the heat and scatter with the berries.

Pour the egg mixture over the fruit in the pan and immediately put in the oven. Bake until puffed and golden, about 18 minutes.

Remove the pancake from the oven and sift confectioners' sugar over the top. Cut into wedges to serve. If desired, offer lemon wedges on the side.

serves four | per serving: calories 309 (kilojoules 1,298), protein 8 g, carbohydrates 34 g, total fat 16 g, saturated fat 9 g, cholesterol 193 mg, sodium 59 mg, dietary fiber 3 g

chorizo and spinach scramble

This version of an old San Francisco dish called Joe's Special is made with spicy Mexican sausage, eggs, and cheese. Hot Italian sausage or regular pork sausage spiked with a little cayenne pepper can be substituted for the chorizo. Serve with Cabin Potatoes (page 42).

2 tablespoons vegetable oil
¾ lb (375 g) chorizo, thinly sliced (see note)
4 green (spring) onions, including tender green tops, sliced
2 bunches fresh spinach, stems removed and leaves chopped, or 1 package (10 oz/315 g) washed spinach leaves, chopped
6 eggs
2 tablespoons warm water
1 cup (4 oz/125 g) shredded Monterey jack cheese

In a large frying pan over medium-high heat, warm the oil. Add the sausage and cook, stirring often, until browned, about 5 minutes. Drain off the fat. Add the green onions and cook until softened, about 2 minutes. Add the chopped spinach in batches, stirring after each addition to wilt the leaves. Once all the spinach has been added and cooked down, pour off any liquid in the bottom of the pan.

In a bowl, beat the eggs with the warm water and cheese. Pour over the spinach-sausage mixture and cook, stirring, until the eggs are softly scrambled. Serve immediately.

serves four | per serving: calories 697 (kilojoules 2,927), protein 41 g, carbohydrates 8 g, total fat 56 g, saturated fat 20 g, cholesterol 424 mg, sodium 1,397 mg, dietary fiber 4 g

cabin potatoes

This potato cake (photo page 41) is crisp outside, creamy within, and easy to prepare. If you don't have a nonstick frying pan, simply use a regular one and add more butter to prevent sticking. Top wedges of the cake with sour cream and smoked fish, or a dollop of applesauce.

4 large baking potatoes, about 3 lb (1.5 kg) total weight
1 small red (Spanish) onion
salt and ground pepper
4 tablespoons (2 oz/60 g) unsalted butter

Peel, then shred the potatoes. Place in a large bowl. Grate the onion into the potatoes. Season generously with salt and pepper and stir to mix well.

Melt 2 tablespoons of the butter in a 10- to 12-inch (25- to 30-cm) nonstick frying pan over medium-high heat. Add the potato-onion mixture and spread in an even layer, pressing it down to make a cake. Cut a piece of aluminum foil large enough to cover the entire surface and set on the mixture. Place a heatproof plate, top side down, directly on the foil. (It should be just slightly smaller than the pan circumference.) Cook the potatoes, undisturbed, until the bottom is well browned, 12–15 minutes.

Remove the plate and foil. Holding the plate and the pan with hot pads, invert them so that the potato cake turns, browned side up, onto the plate. Return the pan to the heat and melt the remaining 2 tablespoons butter. Slide the potatoes, browned side up, into the pan. Replace the foil and the plate and continue to cook, undisturbed, until well browned on the second side, about 10 minutes longer. Remove from the heat, remove the plate and foil, and slide the potato cake onto a serving plate. Cut into wedges to serve.

serves six | per serving: calories 218 (kilojoules 916), protein 4 g, carbohydrates 34 g, total fat 8 g, saturated fat 5 g, cholesterol 21 mg, sodium 15 mg, dietary fiber 3 g

overnight carrot muffins

These light, wholesome muffins offer ultra convenience. The batter can be made up to 2 days ahead. Or, if you prefer, bake the muffins right away, decreasing the cooking time by 5 minutes.

2 cups (10 oz/315 g) all-purpose (plain) flour
1 cup (3 oz/90 g) rolled oats
1 cup (7 oz/220 g) firmly packed light brown sugar
2 teaspoons baking soda (bicarbonate of soda)
½ teaspoon salt
½ teaspoon ground allspice
1 cup (6 oz/185 g) raisins
2 eggs
1 cup (8 fl oz/250 ml) buttermilk
½ cup (4 fl oz/125 ml) vegetable oil
1 cup (5 oz/155 g) lightly packed shredded carrots

In a large bowl, stir together the flour, oats, brown sugar, baking soda, salt, and allspice. Add the raisins and toss to coat with the flour mixture. In another bowl, beat the eggs, buttermilk, oil, and carrots until well blended. Pour over the flour-raisin mixture and stir just until blended; do not overmix. Cover tightly and refrigerate overnight, or for up to 2 days.

To bake, preheat an oven to 375°F (190°C). Oil 12 standard muffin pan cups. Spoon the batter into the prepared cups and bake until golden brown and a toothpick inserted in the center of a muffin comes out clean, about 25 minutes. Remove from the oven and let cool in the pan on a rack for about 5 minutes. Serve warm or transfer the muffins to the rack to cool completely.

makes twelve muffins | per muffin: calories 336 (kilojoules 1,411), protein 6 g, carbohydrates 52 g, total fat 12 g, saturated fat 2 g, cholesterol 37 mg, sodium 335 mg, dietary fiber 2 g

lunch

stuffed summer sandwich

If you prefer a vegetarian version of this portable sandwich, replace the ham with sliced mozzarella, Monterey jack cheese, or grilled eggplant. The loaf can be covered in plastic wrap, refrigerated overnight, and sliced just before serving.

2 large red bell peppers (capsicums)
1 round loaf sourdough or coarse country bread
1 can (6 oz/185 g) pitted black olives, drained
1 clove garlic
2 tablespoons olive oil
½ lb (250 g) thinly sliced baked ham or prosciutto
1 large ripe tomato, thinly sliced
1 cup (1 oz/30 g) packed fresh basil leaves or 4–6 leaves of red-leaf lettuce

Preheat a broiler (griller). Cut the bell peppers into quarters and remove the stems, seeds, and ribs. Place the quarters, cut sides down, on a baking sheet and broil (grill) about 4 inches (10 cm) below the heat until the skins blacken and blister. Transfer to a paper bag and seal; let steam until cool enough to handle. Peel off and discard the skins. Set the peppers aside.

Place the bread on a cutting board and, with the tip of a serrated knife, cut a large circle in the top about ½ inch (12 mm) deep and 1 inch (2.5 cm) from the edge. Pull out the circle of crust; remove all of the bread attached to it to make a lid. Pull out all of the bread from the interior of the loaf, leaving a shell ½ inch (12 mm) thick. Set the bread shell and lid aside. (Reserve the pulled-out bread for another use.)

In a blender or food processor, combine the olives, garlic, and olive oil; process until fairly smooth. Using a rubber spatula, spread the olive paste around the inside of the bread shell and on the underside of the bread lid. (Alternatively, mince the olives and garlic, place in a small bowl and stir in the olive oil to make a coarse paste. Spread the olive paste on the bottom of the bread shell.) Line the bread shell with half of the ham or prosciutto. Top with half of the roasted pepper quarters, then half of the tomato slices, and a few basil leaves or 2 or 3 lettuce leaves. Use just enough to cover the filling without overlapping too much. Repeat the layers, ending with basil or lettuce. Replace the bread lid and press down lightly to compact the layers. Cut into wedges and serve.

serves six | per serving: calories 366 (kilojoules 1,537), protein 16 g, carbohydrates 45 g, total fat 13 g, saturated fat 3 g, cholesterol 22 mg, sodium 1,280 mg, dietary fiber 4 g

chicken caesar salad

This Caesar features an eggless dressing, perfect for a warm-weather lunch by the lake. If you prefer, grill the bruschetta (toasted bread) and the chicken over hot coals. If desired, accompany with Spiced Lentil and Rice Soup (page 50).

4 skinless, boneless chicken breast halves, about 1½ lb (750 g) total weight
½ cup (4 oz/125 ml) lemon juice
1½ tablespoons Worcestershire sauce
1 tablespoon Dijon mustard
8 tablespoons (4 fl oz/125 ml) extra-virgin olive oil
8 slices crusty Italian or sourdough bread
1 or 2 cloves garlic
1 head romaine (cos) lettuce, leaves separated and torn into pieces
¾ cup (3 oz/90 g) grated Parmesan or aged Asiago cheese
1 anchovy fillet in olive oil (optional)
ground pepper

Place the chicken breasts in a nonaluminum container. In a small bowl, whisk together the lemon juice, Worcestershire sauce, and mustard. Whisk in 2 tablespoons of the olive oil. Pour half of this mixture over the chicken breasts, turn to coat well, then cover and marinate for up to 1 hour at room temperature or up to 4 hours in the refrigerator. Set the remaining mixture aside.

Preheat a broiler (griller). Arrange the bread slices on a broiler pan and broil (grill) about 4 inches (10 cm) below the heat, turning once, until golden brown on both sides, about 4 minutes total. Remove from the broiler and immediately brush one side of each slice with some of the remaining olive oil, then rub the same side with a garlic clove. Set the bruschetta aside. Place the chicken breasts on the same broiler pan and broil, turning once, until golden brown on the outside and no longer pink in the center when cut, about 15 minutes total. Remove from the broiler and slice each breast crosswise into strips, keeping the slices together.

Place the lettuce in a large bowl. Add the cheese and toss lightly. Whisk the remaining olive oil with the reserved lemon juice–mustard mixture. If desired, mash the anchovy fillet into the dressing. Pour over the lettuce, season liberally with pepper, and toss well. Divide the salad among individual plates. Top each portion with a sliced chicken breast and garnish with 2 bruschetta slices, then serve.

serves four | per serving: calories 654 (kilojoules 2,747), protein 54 g, carbohydrates 27 g, total fat 36 g, saturated fat 9 g, cholesterol 116 mg, sodium 871 mg, dietary fiber 4 g

spiced lentil and rice soup

Lentils, which don't have to be presoaked, cook relatively fast, making this a quick-to-fix soup (photo page 48).

about 1¼ cups (12 oz/375 g) dried brown lentils
2 tablespoons vegetable oil
1 large yellow or red (Spanish) onion, chopped
2 large carrots, chopped
½ cup (3½ oz/105 g) long-grain white rice
1½ tablespoons good-quality curry powder
8 cups (64 fl oz/2 l) chicken or vegetable broth, plus broth as needed
salt and ground pepper
½ cup (4 oz/125 g) plain nonfat yogurt
½ teaspoon ground cumin

Rinse the lentils in a fine-mesh sieve and discard any stones or debris.

In a deep, heavy pot, warm the oil over medium-high heat. Add the onion and carrots and cook, stirring, until the onion is soft, about 5 minutes. Stir in the rice, curry powder, and lentils. Stir until the mixture is fragrant and the beans and rice are coated with oil, about 2 minutes. Add the 8 cups (64 fl oz/2 l) broth, cover, and bring to a boil. Stir again, then reduce the heat to low, and simmer, covered, until the lentils and rice are cooked through, about 30 minutes.

Remove from the heat and let stand for about 10 minutes before serving. Season well with salt and pepper. (Or let cool, covered, and refrigerate for up to 24 hours. Reheat before serving; if the soup becomes too thick, thin first with a little more broth.)

In a small bowl, blend the yogurt and cumin. Ladle the soup into bowls and drizzle a little yogurt on top of each portion.

serves six | per serving: calories 386 (kilojoules 1,621), protein 22 g, carbohydrates 57 g, total fat 8 g, saturated fat 1 g, cholesterol 0 mg, sodium 1,373 mg, dietary fiber 9 g

the ultimate blt

Not much beats an old standby made with the best ingredients possible. Basil substitutes for lettuce; its sharp herbal taste is the perfect balance to the sweet bacon. If basil is unavailable, use good-quality lettuce.

8 slices Brown Sugar Bacon (page 25)
8 slices coarse country bread
1 cup (4 oz/125 g) grated Vermont or other sharp cheddar cheese
3 tablespoons mayonnaise
1 large ripe red or yellow tomato, cored and sliced
32 fresh basil leaves (see note)

Preheat a broiler (griller). Place a double piece of aluminum foil large enough to hold all the bread slices on a broiler pan and arrange the bread slices on top. Toast the bread until golden on one side, about 2 minutes. Turn and top 4 of the slices with the cheese, dividing it evenly. Continue to toast until the cheese is melted and the other 4 slices are golden on the second side, about 2 minutes. Remove from the broiler.

Spread the plain bread slices with the mayonnaise. Place 2 strips of bacon, broken in half, atop each slice. Cover with the tomato slices, then the basil leaves, distributing them as evenly as possible. Invert the slices with melted cheese onto the slices with the basil. Cut the sandwiches in half and serve immediately.

serves four | per sandwich: calories 538 (kilojoules 2,260), protein 20 g, carbohydrates 43 g, total fat 32 g, saturated fat 12 g, cholesterol 56 mg, sodium 974 mg, dietary fiber 3 g

cheese toasts with celery root–carrot salad

Because carrots and celery root last so long in the refrigerator, this is a good choice to serve at the end of a week's stay at a cabin. If you can get your hands on some fresh herbs, toss them in to brighten the flavor.

¼ cup (2 fl oz/60 ml) sherry wine vinegar or red wine vinegar
1 tablespoon Dijon mustard
⅓ cup (3 fl oz/80 ml) extra-virgin olive oil
4 large carrots, about 1½ lb (750 g) total weight, shredded
1 celery root (celeriac)
salt and ground pepper
chopped fresh tarragon, chervil, or parsley (optional)
4 large slices coarse country bread, each about ½ inch (12 mm) thick
1 cup (4 oz/125 g) shredded Gruyère or Swiss cheese

Preheat a broiler (griller). In a small bowl, whisk together the vinegar and mustard. Pour in the oil, whisking constantly, until blended. Set aside.

Place the shredded carrots in a serving bowl. Using a large, sharp knife, cut off the peel from the celery root and trim away any brown spots. Cut the celery root into quarters and shred. Add to the bowl with the carrots. Pour the dressing over the shredded vegetables and toss well. Season to taste with salt and pepper and toss in the chopped fresh herbs, if using. Set aside.

Arrange the bread slices on a broiler (griller) pan and broil (grill) about 4 inches (10 cm) below the heat until golden on one side, about 2 minutes. Turn and top evenly with the cheese. Broil until the cheese melts, about 2 minutes. Transfer the cheese toasts to individual plates and spoon a little of the celery root–carrot salad evenly over the tops. Serve the remaining salad on the side.

serves four | per serving: calories 474 (kilojoules 1,991), protein 14 g, carbohydrates 42 g, total fat 29 g, saturated fat 8 g, cholesterol 31 mg, sodium 518 mg, dietary fiber 6 g

tortilla soup with lime

If you can't find canned hominy, substitute fresh or thawed frozen corn kernels and add them with the tomatoes.

6 corn tortillas
salt
6 cups (48 fl oz/1.5 l) chicken broth
1 can (15 oz/470 g) yellow hominy, drained and rinsed (see note)
½ cup (2½ oz/75 g) finely chopped red (Spanish) onion
½ teaspoon ground cumin
½ teaspoon dried oregano
2 firm, ripe plum (Roma) tomatoes, seeded and diced
juice of 2 limes
2 ripe avocados, pitted, peeled, and cubed
sprigs of fresh cilantro (fresh coriander)
about ¼ cup (2 oz/60 g) sour cream or nonfat plain yogurt

Preheat an oven to 350°F (180°C). Dip each tortilla into a bowl of cold water, then sprinkle with salt. Stack the tortillas and cut into thin strips, then cut the strips in half crosswise. Scatter the tortilla strips on a large baking sheet and bake until crisp, about 15 minutes.

Meanwhile, in a large saucepan, combine the broth, hominy, onion, cumin, and oregano. Bring to a boil, then reduce the heat to low and simmer, covered, until the onion is tender, about 15 minutes. Add the tomatoes and lime juice, return the soup to a boil, then remove from the heat.

Remove the tortilla strips from the oven. Ladle the soup into bowls and top each portion with some of the hot strips. Accompany with the avocado cubes, cilantro sprigs, and sour cream or yogurt in small serving bowls.

serves four | per serving: calories 414 (kilojoules 1,739), protein 10 g, carbohydrates 45 g, total fat 23 g, saturated fat 5 g, cholesterol 6 mg, sodium 1,806 mg, dietary fiber 7 g

greek rice salad

Rice is the basis for a filling lunch salad that's easy to take on a picnic. Make it a day ahead so the flavors have a chance to develop.

3 cups (24 fl oz/750 ml) water
½ teaspoon salt
1½ cups (10½ oz/330 g) long-grain white rice
¾ cup (6 fl oz/180 ml) lemon juice
1 tablespoon Dijon mustard
½ cup (4 fl oz/125 ml) extra-virgin olive oil
2 tablespoons chopped fresh oregano or 1 tablespoon dried oregano
6 oz (185 g) feta cheese, crumbled
6 oz (185 g) Kalamata or other brine-cured olives, halved and pitted
about 1 lb (500 g) red or yellow cherry tomatoes, cut in half if large
1 cucumber, peeled, seeded, and diced
½ cup (½ oz/15 g) packed fresh mint leaves or parsley leaves, coarsely chopped

In a saucepan, combine the water and salt and bring to a boil. Add the rice, reduce the heat to low, cover, and simmer until the rice is tender and the water is absorbed, about 20 minutes.

Meanwhile, in a large salad bowl, whisk together the lemon juice and mustard. Add the oil, whisking constantly until blended. Stir in the oregano. Add the feta, olives, tomatoes, and cucumber and toss well. Set aside.

When the rice is done, place it in a fine-mesh sieve and rinse with cold running water until cool. Drain well, shaking out the excess water. Add to the salad bowl and toss gently to combine. Add the mint or parsley and toss again. Serve or cover and refrigerate for up to 24 hours.

serves four to six | per serving: calories 629 (kilojoules 2,642), protein 10 g, carbohydrates 62 g, total fat 38 g, saturated fat 9 g, cholesterol 30 mg, sodium 1,219 mg, dietary fiber 2 g

farfalle with chickpeas and winter vegetables

Two favorite Italian sauces—bacony *amatriciana* and bean-and-tomato *pasta e fagioli*—are combined for this robust dish. *Farfalle* means "butterflies" (also called bow ties). You can use other bite-sized pasta shapes if you prefer.

1 tablespoon olive oil
2 slices thick-cut bacon, chopped
1 yellow onion, chopped
2 carrots, chopped
3 celery stalks, sliced
1 large can (28 oz/875 g) peeled and chopped tomatoes
1 can (15 oz/470 g) chickpeas (garbanzo beans), drained and rinsed
ground pepper
1 lb (500 g) farfalle (see note)
about ½ cup (2 oz/60 g) grated Parmesan or aged Asiago cheese

In a large frying pan, warm the oil over medium-high heat. Add the bacon and cook, stirring often, until browned, about 5 minutes. Add the onion, carrots, and celery. Cook, stirring often, until the vegetables are softened, about 5 minutes. Add the tomatoes and chickpeas, stir well, and bring to a boil. Reduce the heat to low and simmer, uncovered, until the sauce is thickened and the flavors have melded, about 15 minutes. Season to taste with pepper.

Meanwhile, bring a large pot two-thirds full of salted water to a boil over high heat. Add the pasta, stir well, and cook until al dente (tender but firm to the bite), about 12 minutes or according to the package directions. Drain the pasta and return to the pot or to a warmed large bowl. Add the tomato-chickpea sauce and toss well. Serve at once with the grated cheese.

serves four | per serving: calories 761 (kilojoules 3,196), protein 28 g, carbohydrates 113 g, total fat 22 g, saturated fat 7 g, cholesterol 22 mg, sodium 846 mg, dietary fiber 9 g

pizza with gorgonzola, potatoes, and rosemary

1 package (2½ teaspoons) active dry yeast
¾ cup (6 fl oz/180 ml) lukewarm water (105°–115°F/40°–46°C)
2½ cups (12½ oz/390 g) all-purpose (plain) flour
½ teaspoon salt
3 tablespoons olive oil
3 red potatoes, about 1 lb (500 g) total weight
cornmeal for dusting
2 oz (60 g) gorgonzola cheese or 4 oz (125 g) blue cheese
leaves from 1 fresh rosemary sprig, chopped, or 2 teaspoons dried oregano

In a measuring cup, sprinkle the yeast over the warm water. Add a pinch of flour, stir, and let stand until foamy, about 10 minutes.

In a bowl, stir together the flour and salt. Pour in the yeast mixture and 1 tablespoon of the olive oil and mix with a fork until the dough forms. Turn out onto a floured work surface and knead until smooth and elastic, about 5 minutes. Form into a ball and place in an oiled bowl; cover with plastic wrap and let rise in a warm place until doubled in bulk, about 1 hour.

Meanwhile, place the potatoes in a saucepan, add cold water to cover, salt lightly, and bring to a boil over high heat. Boil until tender when pierced, about 20 minutes. Drain and, when cool enough to handle, peel. Set aside.

Position a rack in the lower third of an oven and preheat to 450°F (230°C). Punch down the dough and turn out onto the floured work surface. Knead once or twice to expel the air. Using a rolling pin, roll the dough out to an 8-inch (20-cm) round. With your fingers, push and extend the dough out into a round about 10 inches (25 cm) in diameter, pinching up the edge to form a rim around the perimeter. Dust a baking sheet with cornmeal and transfer the dough to it. Brush the top of the dough with 1 tablespoon of the olive oil.

Slice the cooked potatoes as thinly as possible and arrange, slightly overlapping, in concentric circles on top of the pizza. Crumble the cheese evenly over the potatoes. Sprinkle the rosemary or oregano over the cheese. Drizzle with the remaining 1 tablespoon olive oil. Bake until the crust is golden brown and the cheese is bubbly, about 25 minutes. Remove from the oven, slide onto a cutting board, cut into wedges, and serve.

serves four | per serving: calories 574 (kilojoules 2,411), protein 15 g, carbohydrates 92 g, total fat 16 g, saturated fat 5 g, cholesterol 12 mg, sodium 480 mg, dietary fiber 5 g

grilled eggplant caprese

Adding grilled eggplant slices and a side of toasted bread to the classic *caprese* trio—mozzarella, basil, and ripe tomatoes—makes it a complete summer lunch. If whole-milk mozzarella is unavailable, substitute goat cheese or sprinkle the vegetables with feta.

2 large eggplants (aubergines), thinly sliced
about ⅓ cup (3 fl oz/80 ml) extra-virgin olive oil
1 loaf coarse country bread, sliced
8 oz (250 g) fresh whole-milk mozzarella cheese, thinly sliced (see note)
1 lb (500 g) ripe tomatoes, thinly sliced
about 24 large fresh basil leaves
3 tablespoons balsamic vinegar
salt and ground pepper

Prepare a fire in a grill or preheat a broiler (griller).

If using a grill, when the coals are hot, brush one side of each eggplant slice with olive oil and place, oiled side down, on the grill rack. Cook the slices until well browned on one side, brush with more olive oil, turn, and cook until well browned on the second side, about 10 minutes total.

If using a broiler, brush a baking sheet lightly with oil. Brush one side of each eggplant slice with olive oil and place, oiled side up, on the sheet. Broil (grill) about 4 inches (10 cm) below the heat until well browned on top, then turn, brush with oil, and broil until well browned on the second side, about 10 minutes total.

Remove the eggplant from the grill or broiler and let cool. Repeat the procedure with the bread slices and oil, brushing each side with oil and grilling or broiling until golden brown on both sides, about 5 minutes total.

When the eggplant is cool, arrange on a platter with the cheese and tomato slices. Stack the basil leaves and roll them up like a cigar; cut crosswise into thin shreds. Scatter the basil over the vegetables and cheese, then drizzle with the balsamic vinegar. Season to taste with salt and pepper. Offer the toasted bread alongside.

serves four | per serving: calories 696 (kilojoules 2,923), protein 24 g, carbohydrates 74 g, total fat 35 g, saturated fat 11 g, cholesterol 44 mg, sodium 892 mg, dietary fiber 8 g

warm cannellini salad with tuna and sage

Beans and tuna—two ingredients that keep indefinitely when canned—are combined in a rustic salad with Tuscan overtones. Offer the salad with toasted slices of crusty bread and a crisp white wine.

juice of 2 large lemons
2 teaspoons Dijon mustard
½ small red (Spanish) onion, finely chopped
4 celery stalks, halved lengthwise and thinly sliced
1 can (6 oz/185 g) chunk white tuna packed in spring water, drained
¼ cup (2 fl oz/60 ml) extra-virgin olive oil
2 heaping tablespoons chopped fresh sage or 2½ teaspoons dried sage
2 cans (15 oz/470 g each) cannellini beans, drained and well rinsed
salt and ground pepper

In a large bowl, stir together the lemon juice and mustard until the mustard dissolves completely. Add the onion and celery and mix well. Gently stir in the tuna.

In a large frying pan over medium heat, warm the oil and sage until the oil is hot and the sage starts to sizzle. Add the beans and cook, stirring once or twice, until hot, about 3 minutes. Add to the bowl with the tuna and stir to coat. Season to taste with salt and pepper. Serve warm.

serves four | per serving: calories 347 (kilojoules 1,457), protein 22 g, carbohydrates 29 g, total fat 16 g, saturated fat 2 g, cholesterol 17 mg, sodium 508 mg, dietary fiber 9 g

fast french onion soup

This traditional bistro favorite is a great addition to your cabin repertoire. It's warming and filling and made with ingredients you can always keep on hand. In addition to lunch, it also makes for a light supper after a late-night arrival.

1 tablespoon unsalted butter
1 tablespoon olive oil
2 yellow onions, sliced
1 leek, including about 1 inch (2.5 cm) of green, sliced, or 1 yellow onion, sliced
1 cup (8 fl oz/250 ml) dry white wine, such as sauvignon blanc or Sancerre
1 teaspoon sugar
½ teaspoon dried thyme
12 slices crusty baguette or 2 hard rolls, cut into 12 slices
¾ cup (3 oz/90 g) grated Gruyère, Swiss, or aged Asiago cheese
3 cups (24 fl oz/750 ml) beef broth
3 cups (24 fl oz/750 ml) chicken broth
ground pepper

In a large saucepan over high heat, melt the butter with the oil. Add the onions and the leek or additional onion and cook, stirring, until softened, about 7 minutes. Add the wine, sugar, and thyme and bring to a boil. Reduce the heat to medium-high and cook, stirring occasionally, until the onions are very soft, about 10 minutes.

Meanwhile, preheat a broiler (griller). Place the bread slices on a double layer of aluminum foil. Slip under the broiler about 4 inches (10 cm) below the heat and broil (grill) until golden on one side, about 2 minutes. Turn and top the bread evenly with the cheese; broil until the cheese is melted, about 2 minutes. Remove from the broiler and set aside.

Add the beef and chicken broth to the onions, cover, and bring to a boil. Reduce the heat to low and simmer, covered, for 5 minutes longer. Remove the soup from the heat and season well with pepper. Ladle into bowls, float 2 or 3 cheese toasts atop each serving, and serve immediately.

serves four to six | per serving: calories 322 (kilojoules 1,352), protein 12 g, carbohydrates 30 g, total fat 14 g, saturated fat 6 g, cholesterol 25 mg, sodium 1,386 mg, dietary fiber 2 g

dinner

chicken pot pie

for the crust:

1 cup (5 oz/155 g) all-purpose (plain) flour
2 tablespoons grated Parmesan cheese
pinch of salt
7 tablespoons unsalted butter, chilled, cut into small pieces
3–4 tablespoons milk

for the filling:

2 tablespoons unsalted butter
1 leek, sliced
1 large carrot, chopped
1 sweet potato or baking potato, peeled and diced
1 tablespoon all-purpose (plain) flour
2 cups (16 fl oz/500 ml) chicken broth
2 cups (about ½ lb/250 g) cubed cooked chicken or turkey
1 cup (5 oz/155 g) peas (fresh or thawed frozen)
1 cup (8 fl oz/250 ml) half-and-half (half cream)
¼ cup (⅓ oz/10 g) chopped fresh parsley
½ teaspoon dried tarragon
salt and ground pepper

Preheat an oven to 400°F (200°C). To make the crust, in a bowl, stir together the flour, Parmesan, and salt. Using 2 knives or a pastry blender, cut in the butter until the mixture resembles coarse meal. Pour in 3 tablespoons of the milk and mix quickly with a fork until moistened; if the dough seems dry, add the remaining 1 tablespoon milk. Turn out onto a lightly floured work surface and gather together. Knead briefly until the dough just holds together. Enclose in plastic wrap and chill.

To make the filling, in a saucepan, melt the butter over medium-high heat. Add the leek, carrot, and potato and cook, stirring, until the leek is softened, about 5 minutes. Add the flour and stir for 1 minute. Stir in the broth. Bring to a boil, then reduce the heat to low and simmer until slightly thickened, about 3 minutes. Stir in the chicken or turkey, peas, half-and-half, parsley, and tarragon. Simmer until slightly thickened, about 5 minutes longer. Season to taste with salt and pepper. Spoon the filling into a deep 2-qt (2-l) baking dish.

On a lightly floured surface, roll out the dough to fit the inside dimensions of the dish. Trim off any rough edges. Place the dough on top of the filling. Bake until the crust is golden brown, 35–40 minutes. Serve at once.

serves four | per serving: calories 693 (kilojoules 2,911), protein 28 g, carbohydrates 55 g, total fat 40 g, saturated fat 22 g, cholesterol 146 mg, sodium 686 mg, dietary fiber 5 g

winter pot roast

Just a handful of ingredients adds up to a tender, savory dinner. Serve each helping over mashed potatoes or wide egg noodles tossed with butter and chopped parsley.

1 boneless chuck roast, 3½–4 lb (1.75–2 kg), at room temperature
¼ cup (2 fl oz/60 ml) olive oil
2 lb (1 kg) yellow onions, thinly sliced
1 bottle (750 ml) full-bodied red wine
2 tablespoons tomato paste
salt and ground pepper

Preheat an oven to 350°F (180°C).

Pat the meat dry with paper towels. In a Dutch oven or other large, heavy pot with a lid, warm the olive oil over medium-high heat. When the oil is hot but not smoking, place the meat in the pot and brown on all sides, turning with a large fork and spoon as needed, about 15 minutes. The meat is properly browned when it releases from the pan without sticking.

Transfer the meat to a plate and set aside. Add the onions to the pot and cook, stirring often, until softened, about 10 minutes. Add the wine, tomato paste, and salt and pepper to taste; stir well and bring to a boil. Return the meat and any accumulated juices to the pot and bring to a boil. Spoon some of the liquid and onions over the top of the meat. Cover the pot and transfer it to the oven. Bake until the meat pulls apart easily with a fork, about 2½ hours.

Transfer the meat to a carving board. Cut across the grain into thick slices and arrange on a serving platter or individual plates. Spoon the sauce over the slices and serve at once.

serves six | per serving: calories 872 (kilojoules 3,362), protein 51 g, carbohydrates 16 g, total fat 66 g, saturated fat 24 g, cholesterol 204 mg, sodium 244 mg, dietary fiber 3 g

bean and sausage chili

Modify this recipe according to your taste: use hot sausages for spicy chili or sweet sausages for a milder flavor. If you like, garnish with sour cream, chopped green (spring) onions, and shredded jack or cheddar cheese.

2 tablespoons vegetable oil
1 yellow onion, chopped
2 bell peppers (capsicums), 1 red and 1 green, chopped
2 cloves garlic, minced
1 lb (500 g) ground beef
¾ lb (375 g) hot or sweet Italian sausage, casings removed
2 tablespoons ground cumin
2 tablespoons paprika
1 tablespoon dried oregano
½ teaspoon cayenne pepper
¾ cup (6 oz/180 ml) dark beer, preferably Mexican
1 large can (28 oz/875 g) peeled and chopped tomatoes
2 cans (15 oz/470 g each) red kidney beans, drained

In a large, heavy pot, warm the oil over medium-high heat. Add the onion, bell peppers, and garlic and cook, stirring often, until the bell peppers are soft, about 7 minutes. Add the beef and sausage, stirring to break up the meat. Cook until the meat is no longer pink, about 10 minutes. Drain off any fat.

Stir in the cumin, paprika, oregano, and cayenne and cook for 1 minute. Add the beer and let simmer for 3–4 minutes, then add the tomatoes and beans. Bring the chili to a boil, then reduce the heat to low, cover, and simmer until thickened and the flavors have melded, about 30 minutes. Ladle into warmed bowls and serve at once.

serves four to six | per serving: calories 598 (kilojoules 2,512), protein 37 g, carbohydrates 36 g, total fat 35 g, saturated fat 11 g, cholesterol 94 mg, sodium 990 mg, dietary fiber 9 g

panfried trout with creamy slaw

Fresh trout is dredged in cornmeal, fried in classic streamside fashion, and served with a cool, creamy coleslaw. A food processor fitted with the shredding disk is easiest for shredding the vegetables, although the large holes of a cheese grater will work just fine.

for the slaw:

½ cup (4 oz/125 g) plain nonfat yogurt
¼ cup (2 oz/60 g) mayonnaise
¼ cup (2 fl oz/60 ml) cider vinegar
2 teaspoons cumin seeds
1 small head green cabbage, cored and shredded
2 large carrots, shredded
4 green (spring) onions, including tender green tops, thinly sliced
salt and ground pepper

for the trout:

4 dressed bone-in or boneless trout with heads intact, 6–8 oz (185–250 g) each
½ cup (4 fl oz/125 ml) milk
½ cup (2½ oz/75 g) yellow cornmeal
salt and ground pepper
2 tablespoons unsalted butter
2 tablespoons vegetable oil

To prepare the slaw, in a large salad bowl, whisk together the yogurt, mayonnaise, and vinegar until smooth. Stir in the cumin seeds. Add the cabbage, carrots, and green onions and toss well. Season to taste with salt and pepper. Set aside. The slaw may be made up to 8 hours ahead, covered, and refrigerated until ready to serve.

To prepare the trout, rinse the fish and pat dry inside and out with paper towels. Pour the milk into a pie pan; spread the cornmeal on a plate. Dip both sides of each fish into the milk, letting the excess drip off, then roll in cornmeal to coat, shaking off the excess. Set the fish, without touching each other, on waxed paper or another plate. Sprinkle with salt and pepper.

In a wide, heavy frying pan, melt the butter in the oil over medium-high heat. Add the fish and cook until crisp and browned on one side, 4–5 minutes. Using a large spatula, gently turn and cook until the second side is crisp and the flesh is just opaque throughout (gently open the cavity to check), 5–6 minutes longer. Serve hot with the slaw alongside.

serves four | per serving: calories 512 (kilojoules 2,150), protein 27 g, carbohydrates 31 g, total fat 32 g, saturated fat 8 g, cholesterol 85 mg, sodium 209 mg, dietary fiber 6 g

extra-crusty baked rigatoni with beef ragù

Few meals are as comforting as a pan of baked pasta. Using rigatoni—large ridged tubes—gives you the pleasure of lasagna with less work.

1 lb (500 g) rigatoni
2 tablespoons olive oil, plus oil as needed
1 yellow onion, chopped
2 cloves garlic, chopped
1½ lb (750 g) ground beef
½ cup (¾ oz/20 g) chopped fresh parsley
1 tablespoon dried oregano
1 large can (28 oz/875 g) peeled and chopped tomatoes
1 cup (8 fl oz/250 ml) heavy (double) cream
salt and ground pepper
8 oz (250 g) whole-milk mozzarella cheese, shredded
1 cup (4 oz/125 g) grated Parmesan or aged Asiago cheese

Preheat an oven to 350°F (180°C). Bring a large pot two-thirds full of salted water to a boil. Add the rigatoni, stir well, and cook until al dente (tender but firm to the bite), about 15 minutes or according to the package directions. Drain the rigatoni, place in a large bowl, and toss with a little olive oil to prevent sticking. Set aside.

In the same pot, heat the 2 tablespoons olive oil over medium-high heat. Add the onion and garlic and cook, stirring, until soft, about 5 minutes. Add the beef and cook, stirring to break up the meat, until no pink remains, about 10 minutes. Drain off any fat. Add the parsley, oregano, and tomatoes and stir well. Bring to a boil, then reduce the heat to low and simmer, uncovered, until the tomatoes break down and the flavors have melded, about 20 minutes. Stir in the cream, raise the heat, and return to a boil. Remove from the heat and season to taste with salt and pepper. Return the rigatoni to the pot with the sauce and toss to coat well.

Oil the bottom of a shallow 3-qt (3-l) baking dish. Spread half of the pasta mixture in the bottom of the dish. Sprinkle with half of the mozzarella. Top with the remaining pasta, the remaining mozzarella, and the Parmesan or Asiago. Bake until the sauce is bubbly and the top is crusty and golden brown, about 35 minutes. Remove from the oven, let stand for about 5 minutes, then serve.

serves six | per serving: calories 922 (kilojoules 3,872), protein 45 g, carbohydrates 68 g, total fat 52 g, saturated fat 25 g, cholesterol 165 mg, sodium 1,005 mg, dietary fiber 3 g

tandoori-style grilled chicken legs

You can re-create the intense flavor of Indian chicken baked in a clay oven by soaking whole legs in a spicy yogurt marinade and grilling them on a covered barbecue or under a broiler. Serve with basmati rice and with sliced cucumbers and tomatoes drizzled with vinegar and oil.

½ cup (4 fl oz/125 ml) lime juice
1 hot green chile such as jalapeño or serrano, seeded, or 1 teaspoon red pepper flakes
1½ teaspoons paprika
1 teaspoon cumin seeds
1 teaspoon ground turmeric
2 cloves garlic
1 piece fresh ginger, about 2 inches (5 cm), peeled
1 cup (8 oz/250 g) plain low-fat or nonfat yogurt
6 whole chicken legs, 2½ lb (1.25 kg) total weight
sprigs of fresh cilantro (fresh coriander), optional

In a blender or food processor, combine the lime juice, chile or red pepper flakes, paprika, cumin seeds, turmeric, garlic, ginger, and yogurt. Process until smooth.

Using a sharp knife, cut a few diagonal slashes along the top side of each chicken leg down to the bone (this helps the meat absorb the marinade). Place the legs in a nonaluminum container or in a large lock-top plastic bag. Add the yogurt mixture, turn a few times to coat, then cover the container or seal the bag and refrigerate for at least 4 hours or for up to 24 hours.

Prepare a fire in a grill or preheat a broiler (griller). If using a grill, when the coals are hot, lift the chicken from the marinade, letting the excess drain off. Place, skin sides down, on the grill rack. Cover the grill and open the vents. Grill the chicken, turning once, until the exterior is crisp and the meat is no longer pink near the bone when cut, about 35 minutes total. If using a broiler, place the chicken on a broiler pan and broil (grill) about 6 inches (15 cm) below the heat, turning once, for about 30 minutes total.

Remove the chicken from the grill or broiler and arrange on a serving platter or individual plates. Garnish with cilantro sprigs, if desired.

serves six | per serving: calories 234 (kilojoules 983), protein 25 g, carbohydrates 3 g, total fat 13 g, saturated fat 4 g, cholesterol 87 mg, sodium 96 mg, dietary fiber 0 g

lake fish with tart green sauce

You can use any lean freshwater fish for this recipe, including bass, trout, pike, or perch.

2 green (spring) onions, including tender green tops, finely chopped
2 cups (2 oz/60 g) parsley leaves, finely chopped
⅓ cup (2½ oz/75 g) capers, rinsed and chopped
1 large clove garlic, minced
½ cup (4 fl oz/125 ml) extra-virgin olive oil, plus oil as needed
¼ cup (2 fl oz/60 ml) lemon juice
4–6 fish fillets, about 6 oz (185 g) each (see note)
salt and ground pepper

Preheat a broiler (griller) or prepare a fire in a grill. In a small bowl, stir together the green onions, parsley, capers, garlic, ½ cup (4 fl oz/125 ml) olive oil, and lemon juice. Set aside. The sauce can be made up to 4 hours ahead, covered, and refrigerated until ready to use.

Brush each fillet with olive oil and sprinkle with salt and pepper. If using a broiler, preheat the broiler pan and brush the pan rack with olive oil. If using a grill, oil a piece of double aluminum foil just large enough to hold the fillets in a single layer. Place the fillets, skin sides down (if there is skin), on the rack in the broiler pan or on the foil on the grill rack. Cover, if grilling, and cook, without turning, until the fish is just opaque throughout, about 6 minutes. Transfer the fish to plates and top each serving with a few spoonfuls of the sauce. Pass additional sauce at the table.

serves four to six | per serving: calories 448 (kilojoules 1,882), protein 33 g, carbohydrates 3 g, total fat 34 g, saturated fat 5 g, cholesterol 116 mg, sodium 512 mg, dietary fiber 1 g

beef stew with caramelized onions and amber lager

The ingredients here are basic, but the flavor is rich and complex. Like most stews, it tastes even better reheated the second day. Serve each portion over rice, mashed potatoes, or parsleyed egg noodles, and offer a steamed green vegetable alongside.

¼ cup (2 fl oz/60 ml) vegetable oil
2½ lb (1.25 kg) beef stew meat, preferably chuck, cut into 1-inch (2.5-cm) chunks
1½ lb (750 g) yellow onions, sliced
1 tablespoon unsalted butter
2 teaspoons sugar
2 tablespoons all-purpose (plain) flour
1½ teaspoons dried thyme
3 carrots, sliced
1 bottle (12 fl oz/375 ml) good-quality amber lager or pale ale
1 cup (8 fl oz/250 ml) beef or chicken broth
1 tablespoon tomato paste
salt and ground pepper

In a large, heavy pot, warm the oil over high heat until hot but not smoking. Working in batches, brown the meat well on all sides, 5–7 minutes. Adjust the heat as necessary to keep the meat from scorching. Transfer the browned meat to a plate and repeat until all the meat is browned.

Add the onions and butter to the pot and stir over high heat until the onions start to soften, about 5 minutes. Reduce the heat to medium and sprinkle in the sugar. Continue to cook the onions, stirring occasionally, until golden brown, about 15 minutes. Add the flour, thyme, and carrots and raise the heat to high. Stir for 1 minute, then pour in the lager or ale, letting it come to a vigorous boil. Stir in the broth and tomato paste and return to a boil.

Return the meat and any accumulated juices on the plate to the pot, let the liquid come just to a boil, then reduce the heat to low, cover, and simmer until the meat is tender when pierced and the sauce is slightly thickened, 1½–2 hours. Season to taste with salt and pepper. Serve on warmed individual plates.

serves four to six | per serving: calories 801 (kilojoules 3,364), protein 42 g, carbohydrates 24 g, total fat 59 g, saturated fat 21 g, cholesterol 170 mg, sodium 365 mg, dietary fiber 4 g

alpine fondue

The traditional après-ski dish served in European chalets is best served in a fondue pot. What better place to keep one than at your cabin. If Gruyère cheese is unavailable, use good-quality Swiss cheese.

1 loaf coarse country bread
6 celery stalks, cut into 2-inch (5-cm) lengths
6 red potatoes, about 2 lb (1 kg) total weight, quartered and steamed
2 red bell peppers (capsicums), seeded and cut into wide strips
1 clove garlic, cut in half
1 cup (8 fl oz/250 ml) dry white wine such as sauvignon blanc or Sancerre
1 lb (500 g) Gruyère cheese, cut into cubes (see note)
pinch of cayenne pepper
3 tablespoons kirsch or vodka
1 tablespoon cornstarch (cornflour)
salt and ground white or black pepper

Cut or tear the bread, including the crusts, into 1½-inch (4-cm) chunks. Arrange the bread and cut-up vegetables on a platter and set aside.

Rub the interior of a 1-to 2-qt (1–2-l) heavy saucepan with the cut sides of the garlic clove. Place the pan over medium-high heat, add the wine, and bring to a boil. Reduce the heat to low and add the cheese and cayenne. Cook, stirring often with a wooden spoon, until the cheese melts, about 10 minutes; it's essential to keep the heat steady so that the mixture does not curdle. In a small bowl, blend the kirsch or vodka and cornstarch, then stir into the fondue. Stir until the mixture is smooth, 3–5 minutes. Season to taste with salt and pepper.

Warm a fondue pot by filling it with boiling water, then dry. Pour the fondue into the pot and set over a flame. (Alternatively, serve the fondue in a warmed ceramic serving dish and place on an electric warmer at the table.) Use fondue forks or long skewers to dip the bread and vegetables into the fondue.

serves four | per serving: calories 1,059 (kilojoules 4,448), protein 49 g, carbohydrates 108 g, total fat 41 g, saturated fat 22 g, cholesterol 125 mg, sodium 1,118 mg, dietary fiber 9 g

grilled leg of lamb with mint raita

A boneless leg of lamb is ideal for summer grilling. If you can't find a leg, substitute six lamb shoulder chops.

for the lamb:

2 cloves garlic, minced
1 tablespoon paprika
2 teaspoons ground cumin
1 teaspoon ground coriander
½ teaspoon vegetable oil
2 teaspoons red wine vinegar
1 teaspoon water
1 butterflied leg of lamb, 2½–3 lb (1.25–1.5 kg)

for the raita:

1 cup (8 oz/250 g) plain nonfat yogurt
1 large ripe tomato, seeded and diced
½ small cucumber, peeled, seeded, and diced
¼ cup (⅓ oz/10 g) coarsely chopped fresh mint, cilantro (fresh coriander), or parsley
juice of 1 lime

To prepare the lamb, in the bottom of a large nonaluminum bowl, stir together the garlic, paprika, cumin, coriander, oil, vinegar, and water to form a paste. Spoon about half of the mixture onto the underside (the side without fat) of the butterflied leg and spread in an even layer. Place the meat, fat side down, in the remaining spice rub in the bowl and move around to coat with the spices. Cover the bowl tightly and refrigerate for at least 4 hours or for up to 24 hours.

Prepare a fire in a grill. When the coals are hot, lift the meat from the bowl and place, fat side down, on the grill rack. Cook, turning once, until both sides are well browned and the meat is pink when cut into with a knife, or until an instant-read thermometer inserted into the thickest part of the leg registers 130–135°F (54–57°C) for medium-rare, 25–30 minutes total.

Meanwhile, make the raita: In a small bowl, stir together the yogurt, tomato, cucumber, chopped herb, and lime juice until smooth.

When the meat is cooked, transfer to a cutting board and let rest for 5 minutes. Thinly slice across the grain and arrange on a serving platter. Pass the raita at the table.

serves six | per serving: calories 443 (kilojoules 1,861), protein 42 g, carbohydrates 7 g, total fat 26 g, saturated fat 11 g, cholesterol 144 mg, sodium 137 mg, dietary fiber 1 g

baked risotto with butternut squash

3½ cups (28 fl oz/875 ml) chicken or vegetable broth
3 tablespoons olive oil
1 yellow onion, chopped
1½ cups (10½ oz/330 g) Arborio or other short-grain white rice
1 small butternut squash, peeled and cut into ½-inch (12-mm) cubes
½ cup (4 fl oz/125 ml) dry white wine or vermouth
1 cup (4 oz/120 g) grated Parmesan or aged Asiago cheese
ground pepper

Place the broth in a saucepan and bring to a simmer over medium heat. Adjust the heat to maintain a simmer. Preheat an oven to 350°F (180°C).

In a large ovenproof frying pan with a lid, warm the oil over medium-high heat. Add the onion and cook, stirring, until softened, about 5 minutes. Add the rice and squash and stir to coat with the oil. Pour in the wine or vermouth and stir until the liquid is absorbed. Add ½ cup (4 fl oz/125 ml) of the simmering broth and stir until it is absorbed. Continue cooking, adding ½ cup (4 fl oz/125 ml) broth at a time and stirring constantly, until you have used an additional 1½ cups (12 fl oz/375 ml) broth. Total cooking time from when you added the wine will be about 12 minutes.

Add the remaining 1½ cups (12 fl oz/375 ml) broth and bring to a boil, stirring. Remove from the heat and stir in ½ cup (2 oz/60 g) of the cheese. Cover and bake the risotto in the oven until tender, about 20 minutes. Stir in the remaining ½ cup (2 oz/60 g) cheese; let stand, partially covered, for 5 minutes. Season to taste with pepper and serve immediately.

serves four | per serving: calories 593 (kilojoules 2,491), protein 20 g, carbohydrates 81 g, total fat 21 g, saturated fat 7 g, cholesterol 22 mg, sodium 1,412 mg, dietary fiber 4 g

roasted turkey breast with root vegetables

Depending upon how many you're serving, you may be able to get two meals from this generous recipe. Use leftover turkey for sandwiches or in a pot pie (page 66). If any of the vegetables are unavailable, substitute equal amounts of the others in any combination.

1 large bone-in turkey breast half, about 3½ lb (1.75 kg)
1 lb (500 g) sweet potatoes
½ lb (250 g) parsnips
1 large yellow or red (Spanish) onion
1 lb (500 g) white or red potatoes
½ lb (250 g) baby carrots or regular carrots
4 tablespoons (2 fl oz/60 ml) olive oil
1½ teaspoons dried thyme
salt and ground pepper

Place a rack in the lower third of an oven and preheat to 375°F (190°C). Rinse the turkey with cold water and pat dry with paper towels. Set aside.

Peel the sweet potatoes, parsnips, and onion. Cut the sweet potatoes, parsnips, onion, and red or white potatoes into 1-inch (2.5-cm) chunks. If using baby carrots, leave whole; if using regular carrots, cut into 1-inch (2.5-cm) lengths. Spread the vegetables in a large roasting pan. Drizzle with 3 tablespoons of the olive oil and sprinkle with 1 teaspoon of the thyme. Toss the vegetables to coat well with the oil and season to taste with salt and pepper. Push the vegetables toward the sides of the pan, creating a space in the center for the turkey breast. Place the turkey breast in the pan, skin side up, and brush with the remaining 1 tablespoon olive oil. Sprinkle with the remaining ½ teaspoon thyme and salt and pepper to taste.

Roast, stirring the vegetables once or twice, until the meat is no longer pink near the bone when cut in the thickest part and the vegetables are tender, about 1½ hours. Transfer the turkey breast to a serving platter and cover with aluminum foil. Increase the oven temperature to 400°F (200°C) and roast the vegetables until crisp, about 10 minutes longer. Carve the meat from the bone and serve with the roasted vegetables.

serves four to six | per serving: calories 670 (kilojoules 2,814), protein 55 g, carbohydrates 50 g, total fat 27 g, saturated fat 6 g, cholesterol 148 mg, sodium 175 mg, dietary fiber 8 g

ham, cheddar, and potato gratin

This luscious casserole is the perfect antidote to a cold day. Serve with a spinach salad or a big plate of steamed broccoli. Reheat any leftovers for breakfast and top with a poached egg.

1½ cups (12 fl oz/375 ml) chicken broth
½ cup (4 fl oz/125 ml) heavy (double) cream
3 cloves garlic
5 or 6 fresh sage leaves, chopped, or 1 teaspoon dried sage
1 center-cut ham steak, about 1¼ lb (625 g), or 1¼ lb (625 g) good-quality baked ham, cut into slices about ½ inch (12 mm) thick
4 large baking potatoes, about 3 lb (1.5 kg) total weight, peeled and thinly sliced
½ lb (250 g) sharp cheddar cheese, finely shredded
ground pepper

Preheat an oven to 375°F (190°C). Butter a shallow 3-qt (3-l) baking dish.

In a small saucepan, combine the broth, cream, garlic, and sage. Bring to a boil, then reduce the heat to low and simmer, uncovered, for 15 minutes.

Meanwhile, trim any fat from the ham steak, if using, and remove and discard the center bone. Cut the ham steak or baked ham into ½-inch (12-mm) dice. Arrange one-third of the potatoes in a layer on the bottom of the prepared dish. Top with half of the diced ham and one-third of the shredded cheese. Repeat the layers of potatoes, diced ham, and shredded cheese. Top with the remaining potatoes and the remaining cheese.

Remove the broth-cream mixture from the heat. Remove and discard the garlic cloves. Season the broth-cream mixture to taste with pepper and pour over the layered vegetables, distributing it as evenly as possible. Bake, uncovered, until the potatoes are tender when pierced and the top is brown, about 1 hour. Remove from the oven and let stand for about 5 minutes before serving.

serves six | per serving: calories 554 (kilojoules 2,327), protein 32 g, carbohydrates 32 g, total fat 33 g, saturated fat 17 g, cholesterol 117 mg, sodium 1,757 mg, dietary fiber 3 g

grilled flank steak with tomato-corn relish

A no-fail choice for the barbecue, flank steak is fast and easy to cook. If you don't have balsamic vinegar, substitute red wine mixed with 1 tablespoon brown sugar.

½ cup (4 fl oz/125 ml) plus 1 tablespoon balsamic vinegar
4 tablespoons (2 fl oz/60 ml) olive oil
2 cloves garlic, minced
1 tablespoon chopped fresh rosemary or 1 tablespoon dried rosemary
1 flank steak, about 1½ lb (750 g)
8 green (spring) onions
3 ears of corn, husks and silks removed
1 lb (500 g) firm, ripe plum (Roma) tomatoes, cored, halved lengthwise, and seeded
salt

In a nonaluminum container, combine the ½ cup (4 fl oz/125 ml) balsamic vinegar, 2 tablespoons of the oil, the garlic, and the rosemary. Add the steak and turn to coat well. Cover tightly and refrigerate for at least 8 hours or for up to 24 hours.

Prepare a fire in a grill. Remove the steak from the refrigerator and let come to room temperature. Leaving the green onions whole, brush all the vegetables lightly with 1 tablespoon of the olive oil.

When the coals are hot, place the vegetables on the grill. Grill, turning, until the green onions are slightly charred, about 3 minutes; the tomatoes are softened and slightly charred, about 4 minutes; and the corn is blackened in spots and the kernels are tender, about 12 minutes. Set aside.

Place the steak on the grill rack. Grill, turning once, until well browned on both sides and medium-rare in the center, about 10 minutes total, depending on the thickness of the steak.

While steak is cooking, cut the corn kernels off the cobs. Coarsely chop the tomatoes and thinly slice the onions. Place the vegetables in a bowl and drizzle with the 1 tablespoon balsamic vinegar and the remaining 1 tablespoon olive oil. Season to taste with salt and mix well. Remove the steak from the grill and slice thinly across the grain. Serve with the tomato-corn relish.

serves six | per serving: calories 334 (kilojoules 1,403), protein 25 g, carbohydrates 19 g, total fat 18 g, saturated fat 5 g, cholesterol 57 mg, sodium 89 mg, dietary fiber 4 g

fusilli primavera

The best produce of spring and summer is the inspiration for this sauce. If you cannot find a red bell pepper, leave it out rather than use a green bell pepper.

1 lb (500 g) fusilli or other bite-sized pasta shape
about ¾ lb (375 g) asparagus
½ cup (4 fl oz/120 ml) extra-virgin olive oil
3 green (spring) onions, including tender green tops, thinly sliced
1 red bell pepper (capsicum), seeded and diced
2 yellow crookneck squash or zucchini (courgettes), diced
¼ cup (⅓ oz/10 g) packed shredded fresh basil leaves or chopped fresh parsley
1½ teaspoons chopped fresh thyme or ¾ teaspoon dried thyme
grated zest of 1 large lemon
ground pepper
about ½ cup (2 oz/60 g) grated Parmesan cheese

Bring a large pot two-thirds full of salted water to a boil over high heat. Add the pasta, stir well, and cook until al dente (tender but firm to the bite), about 12 minutes or according to the package directions.

Meanwhile, trim any tough ends from the asparagus and discard. Cut the asparagus on the diagonal into 1-inch (2.5-cm) lengths; set aside. In a large frying pan, warm ¼ cup (2 fl oz/60 ml) of the oil over medium-high heat. Add the green onions and red pepper and cook, stirring, until the pepper is softened, about 3 minutes. Add the squash or zucchini and the asparagus and cook, stirring often, until the vegetables are tender-crisp, about 7 minutes. Remove from the heat and stir in the basil or parsley, thyme, and lemon zest.

Drain the pasta and return to the pot. Add the vegetables and the remaining ¼ cup (2 fl oz/60 ml) oil. Season well with pepper and toss until warmed through. Serve at once with the grated Parmesan cheese.

serves four | per serving: calories 754 (kilojoules 3,167), protein 23 g, carbohydrates 93 g, total fat 34 g, saturated fat 7 g, cholesterol 10 mg, sodium 627 mg, dietary fiber 4 g

dessert

spiced pear cake

Dense, moist, and nutty, this cake is superb on a cold day as an afternoon snack or dessert. It's also good for breakfast the next day, rewarmed in a low oven. Use baking pears such as Anjou or Comice.

3 firm, ripe pears, peeled, cored, and diced (see note)
1½ cups (12 oz/375 g) sugar
2 cups (10 oz/315 g) all-purpose (plain) flour
1½ teaspoons baking soda (bicarbonate of soda)
1 teaspoon ground cinnamon
½ teaspoon salt
2 eggs, at room temperature
¾ cup (6 fl oz/180 ml) vegetable oil
2 teaspoons vanilla extract (essence)
1 cup (6 oz/185 g) raisins
½ cup (2 oz/60 g) chopped pecans or walnuts

Place the pears in a large bowl with the sugar; stir, then set aside for 15 minutes. Preheat an oven to 350°F (180°C) and grease a shallow 3-qt (3-l) baking dish.

In another bowl, sift together the flour, baking soda, cinnamon, and salt. Then sift the flour mixture into the bowl containing the pears. Add the eggs, oil, vanilla, raisins, and nuts and mix well. Spread the batter evenly into the prepared dish.

Bake until a toothpick inserted in the center of the cake comes out clean, 50–55 minutes. Remove from the oven and let cool in the pan on a rack. Cut into 12 rectangles to serve.

makes twelve rectangles; serves six to eight | per rectangle: calories 444 (kilojoules 1,865), protein 5 g, carbohydrates 68 g, total fat 19 g, saturated fat 2 g, cholesterol 35 mg, sodium 261 mg, dietary fiber 3 g

warm winter fruit compote

Dried fruits keep well in the pantry and, when cooked, have the intense flavors of their fresh counterparts. Try this compote over ice cream or topped with sour cream or yogurt.

1 lb (500 g) dried Turkish or other apricots
8 oz (250 g) dried cranberries
½ cup (3 oz/90 g) golden raisins (sultanas)
2 firm, ripe pears, preferably Comice or Anjou, peeled, cored, and diced
½ cup (4 oz/125 g) sugar
2 cups (16 fl oz/500 ml) water
1½ cups (12 fl oz/375 ml) white dessert wine such as Moscato, late-harvest Riesling, or Sauternes
1 oz (30 g) crystallized ginger, finely chopped

In a heavy saucepan, combine the apricots, cranberries, raisins, pears, sugar, water, wine, and ginger and bring to a boil over medium-high heat, stirring often, until the sugar dissolves. Reduce the heat to low and simmer, uncovered, stirring occasionally, until the fruit is softened and the liquid is thickened, about 40 minutes.

Serve warm or let cool to room temperature, cover, and refrigerate for up to 1 week. Rewarm gently over low heat before serving.

serves six | per serving: calories 486 (kilojoules 2,041), protein 4 g, carbohydrates 124 g, total fat 1 g, saturated fat 0 g, cholesterol 0 mg, sodium 18 mg, dietary fiber 10 g

banana-oatmeal power cookies

These cookies (photo at left) have it all—nuts, grains, fruit. Their portable size makes them perfect for taking on hikes, bike rides, and all sorts of expeditions.

1 cup (5 oz/155 g) all-purpose (plain) flour
½ cup (1½ oz/45 g) flaked coconut
½ cup (1½ oz/45 g) rolled oats
1 teaspoon baking soda (bicarbonate of soda)
½ teaspoon salt
¼ teaspoon ground cinnamon
¾ cup (6 oz/185 g) firmly packed light brown sugar
6 tablespoons (3 oz/90 g) unsalted butter, at room temperature
1 very ripe banana, mashed
1 egg, at room temperature
½ cup (3 oz/90 g) chopped dried apricots or golden raisins (sultanas)
½ cup (2 oz/60 g) chopped walnuts

Preheat an oven to 325°F (165°C). Lightly grease 1 or 2 baking sheets and set aside.

In a bowl, stir together the flour, coconut, oats, baking soda, salt, and cinnamon. In a large bowl, cream the brown sugar and butter with a wooden spoon until fluffy. Add the banana and egg and beat with a fork until blended. Stir in the flour mixture, about ½ cup (2½ oz/75 g) at a time, then stir in the apricots or raisins and the walnuts.

Spoon the dough by heaping tablespoonfuls onto the prepared baking sheet(s), spacing the cookies about 2 inches (5 cm) apart. Bake until golden brown, 12–15 minutes, switching pan positions halfway through baking if 2 pans were used. Remove from the oven and cool on the baking sheet(s) on a rack for about 5 minutes. Transfer the cookies to the rack to cool completely. The cookies can be stored in an airtight container for up to 3 days.

makes about eighteen cookies; serves six | per cookie: calories 104 (kilojoules 437), protein 2 g, carbohydrates 23 g, total fat 8 g, saturated fat 3 g, cholesterol 22 mg, sodium 146 mg, dietary fiber 1 g

peach-raspberry pie

2 cups (10 oz/315 g) plus 3 tablespoons all-purpose (plain) flour
½ teaspoon salt
⅓ cup (3 oz/90 g) chilled vegetable shortening, cut into small pieces
⅓ cup (3 oz/90 g) chilled unsalted butter, cut into small pieces
7 tablespoons cold water
about 2½ lb (1.25 kg) ripe peaches
1½ pt (12 oz/375 g) raspberries
½ cup (4 oz/125 g) sugar
¾ teaspoon almond extract (essence)
1 egg, lightly beaten

In a bowl, stir together the 2 cups (10 oz/315 g) flour and the salt. Using 2 knives or a pastry blender, cut in the shortening and butter until the mixture resembles coarse meal. Sprinkle with the cold water and stir with a fork until moistened. Turn the dough out onto a lightly floured work surface and gather together. Knead briefly just until the dough holds together. Enclose in plastic wrap and refrigerate for about 20 minutes.

Meanwhile, bring a saucepan three-fourths full of water to a boil. Immerse the peaches in the boiling water for 30 seconds. Remove the peaches with a slotted spoon, and when cool enough to handle, peel off the skin. Pit and slice the peaches. In a bowl, combine the sliced peaches, raspberries, sugar, and the 3 tablespoons flour. Stir until the sugar and flour are dissolved. Let stand at room temperature for about 15 minutes.

Preheat an oven to 375°F (190°C). Cut the dough in half; rewrap one half and return to the refrigerator. On a lightly floured work surface, press the other half into a flat disk. Using a floured rolling pin, roll out to a 12-inch (30-cm) round. Transfer to an 8-inch (20-cm) pie dish. Stir the almond extract into the peach-raspberry mixture, then pour into the dough-lined pie dish. Trim off the excess dough, leaving a 1-inch (2.5-cm) overhang.

Roll out the remaining dough to a 12-inch (30-cm) round. Using a fluted pastry wheel or a knife, cut it into strips 1 inch (2.5 cm) wide. Arrange the strips atop the pie in a lattice pattern. Trim any overhanging dough and press gently on the strips all the way around to seal them to the bottom crust. Crimp as desired. Brush the top with the beaten egg. Bake until the crust is golden and the filling is bubbly, about 45 minutes. Transfer to a rack to cool completely. Serve at room temperature.

serves six to eight | per serving: calories 484 (kilojoules 2,033), protein 6 g, carbohydrates 64 g, total fat 23 g, saturated fat 9 g, cholesterol 57 mg, sodium 168 mg, dietary fiber 5 g

tangerine granita

The great thing about a *granita*, a flavorful Italian ice, is that you don't need an ice-cream machine to make it. Just freeze it in a metal container and scrape the crystals up with a fork. Enjoy this granita by a fire in the winter when tangerines and tangelos are at their peak, or make it any time with fresh orange juice, adding the lemon juice to taste. Serve with Lemon Pudding Squares (page 101), if you like.

¾ cup (6 oz/185 g) sugar
1¾ cups (14 fl oz/430 ml) water
1¼ cups (10 fl oz/310 ml) tangerine or tangelo juice
3 tablespoons lemon juice

In a saucepan over low heat, stir the sugar and water together until the sugar dissolves. Raise the heat to high and bring to a boil; boil for 5 minutes. Remove from the heat and stir in the citrus juices.

Pour into a metal bowl, metal baking pan, or other wide, freezer-safe container. Let stand at room temperature until tepid to the touch. Cover with plastic wrap or a lid and place in the freezer. When the mixture begins to get icy, after about 1½ hours, stir it well with a fork. Return to the freezer. Repeat one or two times until the mixture starts to freeze solid, about 4 hours total.

To serve, scrape the surface of the granita with the tines of a fork to create ice crystals. Scoop up the crystals and serve in a glass, cup, or mug. Store the remaining granita in the freezer for up to 1 week, scraping up the amount needed each time.

makes about one quart (one liter); serves four to six | per serving: calories 160 (kilojoules 672), protein 0 g, carbohydrates 41 g, total fat 0 g, saturated fat 0 g, cholesterol 0 mg, sodium 3 mg, dietary fiber 0 g

plum crumble with hazelnuts

This versatile, nutty topping made with oatmeal and hazelnuts can also be sprinkled over peaches, apricots, and nectarines. When using these fruits, season with cinnamon instead of allspice.

⅔ cup (3½ oz/105 g) hazelnuts (filberts) or walnuts
3 lb (1.5 kg) firm, ripe plums, pitted and sliced
¼ cup (2 oz/60 g) sugar
2 tablespoons cornstarch (cornflour)
½ teaspoon ground allspice
1 tablespoon lemon juice
¾ cup (2½ oz/75 g) rolled oats
½ cup (3½ oz/105 g) firmly packed light brown sugar
5 tablespoons (2½ oz/75 g) chilled unsalted butter, cut into small pieces
vanilla ice cream (optional)

Preheat an oven to 375°F (190°C). Spread the hazelnuts or walnuts in a pie pan and toast until fragrant, about 7 minutes. Remove from the oven and, if using hazelnuts, place in a fine-mesh sieve. Working over a sink, rub the hazelnuts vigorously with a clean kitchen towel, letting the skin slough off against the sieve; do not worry if small bits remain. Lift the nuts from the sieve, discarding the skins. Finely chop the hazelnuts or walnuts.

Place the sliced plums in a large bowl. Sift the sugar, cornstarch, and allspice over the fruit. Add the lemon juice and stir until the fruit is evenly coated with the sugar mixture. Spread the fruit in a shallow 3-qt (3-l) baking dish.

In a bowl, stir together the oats, chopped hazelnuts, and brown sugar. Scatter the butter over the oat mixture and, using 2 knives or a pastry blender, cut in until the butter is in tiny pieces and the mixture looks lumpy. Scatter the topping over the fruit, covering it as evenly as possible.

Bake until the fruit is bubbly and the topping is browned, about 40 minutes. Remove from the oven and let cool for 5 minutes. Serve warm or at room temperature, topped with vanilla ice cream, if desired.

serves six | per serving: calories 462 (kilojoules 1,940), protein 6 g, carbohydrates 66 g, total fat 22 g, saturated fat 7 g, cholesterol 26 mg, sodium 10 mg, dietary fiber 7 g

lemon pudding squares

Even people who rarely bake will be proud of the results when they make this simple recipe (photo page 98): lemon custard on the bottom with a meringuelike top layer. It's the perfect ending to casual meals year-round.

¾ cup (6 oz/185 g) sugar
¼ cup (1½ oz/45 g) all-purpose (plain) flour
2 pinches of salt
3 eggs, separated
1 cup (8 fl oz/250 ml) milk
grated zest of 1 Meyer or other small lemon
⅓ cup (3 fl oz/80 ml) Meyer lemon or other lemon juice

Preheat an oven to 350°F (180°C). Butter an 8-inch (20-cm) square baking pan. Bring a kettle of water to a boil.

In a bowl, stir together the sugar, flour, and 1 pinch of salt. In another bowl, whisk together the egg yolks, milk, lemon zest, and lemon juice. Pour over the flour mixture and stir until smooth. In a third bowl, beat the egg whites with the remaining pinch of salt until they hold stiff peaks. Using a rubber spatula, gently fold the whites into the egg yolk mixture until just a few streaks of white remain.

Pour the batter into the prepared pan and set in a larger baking pan. Place in the oven and pour boiling water into the large pan until it comes about halfway up the sides of the smaller pan.

Bake the pudding until golden brown on top, about 40 minutes. Let cool slightly, then cut into squares and serve warm or at room temperature.

makes nine squares; serves four to six | per square: calories 138 (kilojoules 580), protein 3 g, carbohydrates 25 g, total fat 3 g, saturated fat 1 g, cholesterol 76 mg, sodium 68 mg, dietary fiber 0 g

baked stuffed apples

Here's proof of the staying power of old-fashioned recipes. Don't be shy about serving baked apples any time of day; they're especially good for breakfast.

¼ cup (1 oz/30 g) chopped walnuts
4 good-quality red apples such as Fuji, Braeburn, McIntosh, or Rome Beauty
¼ cup (2 oz/60 g) packed brown sugar
2 tablespoons unsalted butter, at room temperature
½ teaspoon ground cinnamon
¼ cup (3 oz/90 g) honey
½ cup (4 fl oz/125 ml) apple juice

Preheat an oven to 350°F (180°C). Spread the walnuts on a baking sheet and toast in the oven until lightly browned and fragrant, about 7 minutes. Remove from the oven and let cool.

Working from the stem end, use a melon baller to remove the core from each apple, scooping out the stem and seeds and making a deep hole for filling; work to within about ½ inch (12 mm) of the bottom of the apple. (Alternatively, remove the core with an apple corer and widen the hole with a small spoon.) Peel the skin from the top half of each apple.

In a small bowl, blend together the brown sugar, butter, and cinnamon. Mix in the walnuts. Spoon equal amounts of the filling into the centers of the apples. Set the filled apples in an 8-inch (20-cm) square baking pan or other baking pan just large enough to hold them snugly.

In a small pan over medium heat, warm the honey with the apple juice, stirring until the honey dissolves. Pour around the apples. Spoon some of the liquid over the sides of the apples to moisten them, but do not spoon over the tops.

Bake, basting the sides once or twice with the pan juices, until the apples are tender when pierced, about 40 minutes. Remove from the oven, let cool, and serve in bowls with the pan juices spooned over the tops.

serves four | per serving: calories 332 (kilojoules 1,394), protein 1 g, carbohydrates 63 g, total fat 11 g, saturated fat 4 g, cholesterol 16 mg, sodium 9 mg, dietary fiber 4 g

sour-cream shortcakes with fresh berries

These shortcakes are made extra-tender with sour cream. Split and top with berries at their peak of sweetness and a dollop of whipped cream.

for the shortcakes:

2 cups (10 oz/315 g) all-purpose (plain) flour

½ cup (4 oz/125 g) sugar

1 teaspoon baking powder

½ teaspoon baking soda (bicarbonate of soda)

½ teaspoon salt

6 tablespoons (3 oz/90 g) chilled butter, cut into small pieces

1 cup (8 oz/250 g) sour cream

1 egg, at room temperature

for the berries:

1 qt (1 lb/500 g) mixed berries such as blackberries, blueberries, strawberries, and/or raspberries

1–2 tablespoons sugar, or to taste

½ cup (4 fl oz/125 ml) heavy (double) cream

½ teaspoon vanilla extract (essence)

Preheat an oven to 425°F (220°C). Lightly grease a baking sheet. Set aside.

To make the shortcakes, in a bowl, stir together the flour, sugar, baking powder, baking soda, and salt. Using 2 knives or a pastry blender, cut in the butter until the mixture resembles coarse meal. Stir in the sour cream and egg until moistened. Turn the dough out onto a lightly floured work surface and pat into a rough circle (the dough will be sticky). Working with about one-sixth of the dough at a time, shape into rough balls and place about 1 inch (2.5 cm) apart on the prepared baking sheet. Bake until golden brown, about 18 minutes.

Meanwhile, prepare the berries: If using strawberries, slice them. In a bowl, combine the fruit with sugar to taste. Stir, then let stand until ready to use.

Remove the shortcakes from the oven and let cool on the baking sheet on a rack. In a bowl, whip the cream with the vanilla until it holds soft peaks. To serve, split each shortcake in half horizontally with your fingers and place a bottom half on each of 6 individual plates. Top generously with the sugared berries and whipped cream. Replace the top half and serve.

serves six | per serving: calories 564 (kilojoules 2,369), protein 8 g, carbohydrates 69 g, total fat 29 g, saturated fat 17 g, cholesterol 110 mg, sodium 526 mg, dietary fiber 4 g

coffee-coconut sundaes

The sauce is so easy that you can make it in the time it takes to cool the coconut. If you prefer, splash the ice cream with warm Kahlúa instead of the sauce, then top with the toasted coconut.

¼ cup (¾ oz/20 g) flaked coconut
⅓ cup (3 fl oz/80 ml) heavy (double) cream
⅔ cup (4 oz/125 g) semisweet (plain) chocolate chips
2 tablespoons Kahlúa
1 pt (16 oz/500 g) coffee ice cream

Preheat an oven to 350°F (180°C). Spread the coconut in a pie pan and toast, stirring once, until golden brown, 8–10 minutes. Remove from the oven and let cool.

While the coconut is cooling, in a small heavy saucepan, combine the cream and chocolate chips. Place over medium-low heat and cook, stirring, until the chocolate melts, 3–5 minutes. Add the Kahlúa and stir until the sauce is smooth.

Scoop the ice cream into bowls, top with the warm sauce, and sprinkle with toasted coconut. Serve immediately, as the sauce hardens if left to cool completely.

serves six | per serving: calories 253 (kilojoules 1,063), protein 3 g, carbohydrates 26 g, total fat 16 g, saturated fat 10 g, cholesterol 37 mg, sodium 50 mg, dietary fiber 0 g

index

acknowledgments

For her incomparable help in tasting and testing the recipes in this book, the author wishes to thank Katherine Withers Cobbs; and for their inspiration, encouragment, and willingness to eat everything, she wishes to thank John and Sue Ritchie and Sam Whiting. The photography team wishes to thank Sue Fisher King, who kindly lent props for the photography, as well as Richard and Pauline Abbe, Elba Borgen, Sarah Hammond, Finn and Pascale Jorgensen, Lorraine and Jud Puckett, and Hellie Robertson. The publishers would like to thank the following people for their generous assistance and support in producing this book: Vicky Carter, Ken DellaPenta, Jennifer Hanson, Sharilyn Hovind, Lisa Lee, and Jan Newberry.